T0284324

PLAY ON SHAKESPEARE

Julius Caesar

PLAY ON SHAKESPEARE

All's Well That Ends Well	Virginia Grise
Antony and Cleopatra	Christopher Chen
As You Like It	David Ivers
The Comedy of Errors	Christina Anderson
Coriolanus	Sean San José
Cymbeline	Andrea Thome
Edward III	Octavio Solis
Hamlet	Lisa Peterson
Henry IV	Yvette Nolan
Henry V	Lloyd Suh
Henry VI	Douglas P. Langworthy
Henry VIII	Caridad Svich
Julius Caesar	Shishir Kurup
King John	Brighde Mullins
King Lear	Marcus Gardley
Love's Labour's Lost	Josh Wilder
Macbeth	Migdalia Cruz
Measure for Measure	Aditi Brennan Kapil
The Merchant of Venice	Elise Thoron
The Merry Wives of Windsor	Dipika Guha
A Midsummer Night's Dream	Jeffrey Whitty
Much Ado About Nothing	Ranjit Bolt
Othello	Mfoniso Udofia
Pericles	Ellen McLaughlin
Richard II	Naomi Iizuka
Richard III	Migdalia Cruz
Romeo and Juliet	Hansol Jung
The Taming of the Shrew	Amy Freed
The Tempest	Kenneth Cavander
Timon of Athens	Kenneth Cavander
Titus Andronicus	Amy Freed
Troilus and Cressida	Lillian Groag
Twelfth Night	Alison Carey
The Two Gentlemen of Verona	Amelia Roper
The Two Noble Kinsmen	Tim Slover
The Winter's Tale	Tracy Young

Julius Caesar

by
William Shakespeare

Modern verse translation by
Shishir Kurup

Dramaturgy by
Nancy Keystone

ACMRS PRESS
Arizona State University
Tempe, Arizona
2022

———

Publication of Play On Shakespeare is assisted by
generous support from the Hitz Foundation.
For more information, please visit www.playonshakespeare.org

———

Published by ACMRS Press
Arizona Center for Medieval and Renaissance Studies,
Arizona State University, Tempe, Arizona
www.acmrspress.com

Library of Congress Cataloging-in-Publication Data

Names: Kurup, Shishir, author. | Keystone, Nancy, contributor. | Shakespeare,
    William, 1564-1616. Julius Caesar.

Title: Julius Caesar / by William Shakespeare ; modern verse translation by
    Shishir Kurup ; dramaturgy by Nancy Keystone.

Description: Tempe, Arizona : ACMRS Press, 2022. | Series: Play on
    Shakespeare | Summary: "This translation updates Shakespeare's language
    to allow more of the playwright's ideas to come through, opening the
    wonders and blazing relevance of the play's rhetorical brilliance to the
    twenty-first century"-- Provided by publisher.

Identifiers: LCCN 2022037167 (print) | LCCN 2022037168 (ebook) | ISBN
    9780866987936 (paperback) | ISBN 9780866987943 (ebook)

Subjects: LCSH: Caesar, Julius--Assassination--Drama. | Brutus, Marcus
    Junius, 85 B.C.?-42 B.C.--Drama. | Conspiracies--Drama. | Rome--
    History--53-44 B.C.--Drama. | Rome--History--Civil War, 43-31 B.C.--
    Drama. | LCGFT: Historical drama. | Tragedies (Drama)

Classification: LCC PR2878.J7 K87 2022 (print) | LCC PR2878.J7 (ebook) |
    DDC 812/.6--dc23/eng/20220802

LC record available at https://lccn.loc.gov/2022037167

LC ebook record available at https://lccn.loc.gov/2022037168

Printed in the United States of America

We wish to acknowledge our gratitude
for the extraordinary generosity of the
Hitz Foundation

∼

Special thanks to the Play on Shakespeare staff
Lue Douthit, CEO and Creative Director
Kamilah Long, Executive Director
Taylor Bailey, Associate Creative Director and Senior Producer
Summer Martin, Director of Operations
Amrita Ramanan as Senior Cultural Strategist and Dramaturg
Katie Kennedy, Publications Project Manager

∼

Originally commissioned by the
Oregon Shakespeare Festival
Bill Rauch, Artistic Director
Cynthia Rider, Executive Director

PLAY ON SHAKESPEARE

In 2015, the Oregon Shakespeare Festival announced a new commissioning program. It was called "Play on!: 36 playwrights translate Shakespeare." It elicited a flurry of reactions. For some people this went too far: "You can't touch the language!" For others, it didn't go far enough: "Why not new adaptations?" I figured we would be on the right path if we hit the sweet spot in the middle.

Some of the reaction was due not only to the scale of the project, but its suddenness: 36 playwrights, along with 38 dramaturgs, had been commissioned and assigned to translate 39 plays, and they were already hard at work on the assignment. It also came fully funded by the Hitz Foundation with the shocking sticker price of $3.7 million.

I think most of the negative reaction, however, had to do with the use of the word "translate." It's been difficult to define precisely. It turns out that there is no word for the kind of subtle and rigorous examination of language that we are asking for. We don't mean "word for word," which is what most people think of when they hear the word translate. We don't mean "paraphrase," either.

The project didn't begin with 39 commissions. Linguist John McWhorter's musings about translating Shakespeare is what sparked this project. First published in his 1998 book *Word on the Street* and reprinted in 2010 in *American Theatre* magazine, he notes that the "irony today is that the Russians, the French, and other people in foreign countries possess Shakespeare to a much greater extent than we do, for the simple reason that they get to enjoy Shakespeare in the language they speak."

This intrigued Dave Hitz, a long-time patron of the Oregon Shakespeare Festival, and he offered to support a project that looked at Shakespeare's plays through the lens of the English we speak today. How much has the English language changed since Shakespeare? Is it possible that there are conventions in the early modern English of Shakespeare that don't translate to us today, especially in the moment of hearing it spoken out loud as one does in the theater?

How might we "carry forward" the successful communication between actor and audience that took place 400 years ago? "Carry forward," by the way, is what we mean by "translate." It is the fourth definition of *translate* in the Oxford English Dictionary.

As director of literary development and dramaturgy at the Oregon Shakespeare Festival, I was given the daunting task of figuring out how to administer the project. I began with Kenneth Cavander, who translates ancient Greek tragedies into English. I figured that someone who does that kind of work would lend an air of seriousness to the project. I asked him how might he go about translating from the source language of early modern English into the target language of contemporary modern English?

He looked at different kinds of speech: rhetorical and poetical, soliloquies and crowd scenes, and the puns in comedies. What emerged from his tinkering became a template for the translation commission. These weren't rules exactly, but instructions that every writer was given.

First, do no harm. There is plenty of the language that doesn't need translating. And there is some that does. Every playwright had different criteria for assessing what to change.

Second, go line-by-line. No editing, no cutting, no "fixing." I want the whole play translated. We often cut the gnarly bits in

Shakespeare for performance. What might we make of those bits if we understood them in the moment of hearing them? Might we be less compelled to cut?

Third, all other variables stay the same: the time period, the story, the characters, their motivations, and their thoughts. We designed the experiment to examine the language.

Fourth, and most important, the language must follow the same kind of rigor and pressure as the original, which means honoring the meter, rhyme, rhetoric, image, metaphor, character, action, and theme. Shakespeare's astonishingly compressed language must be respected. Trickiest of all: making sure to work within the structure of the iambic pentameter.

We also didn't know which of Shakespeare's plays might benefit from this kind of investigation: the early comedies, the late tragedies, the highly poetic plays. So we asked three translators who translate plays from other languages into English to examine a Shakespeare play from each genre outlined in the *First Folio*: Kenneth took on *Timon of Athens,* a tragedy; Douglas Langworthy worked on the *Henry the Sixth* history plays, and Ranjit Bolt tried his hand at the comedy *Much Ado about Nothing.*

Kenneth's *Timon* received a production at the Alabama Shakespeare in 2014 and it was on the plane ride home that I thought about expanding the project to include 39 plays. And I wanted to do them all at once. The idea was to capture a snapshot of contemporary modern English. I couldn't oversee that many commissions, and when Ken Hitz (Dave's brother and president of the Hitz Foundation) suggested that we add a dramaturg to each play, the plan suddenly unfolded in front of me. The next day, I made a simple, but extensive, proposal to Dave on how to commission and develop 39 translations in three years. He responded immediately with "Yes."

My initial thought was to only commission translators who translate plays. But I realized that "carry forward" has other meanings. There was a playwright in the middle of the conversation 400 years ago. What would it mean to carry *that* forward?

For one thing, it would mean that we wanted to examine the texts through the lens of performance. I am interested in learning how a dramatist makes sense of the play. Basically, we asked the writers to create performable companion pieces.

I wanted to tease out what we mean by contemporary modern English, and so we created a matrix of writers who embodied many different lived experiences: age, ethnicity, gender-identity, experience with translations, geography, English as a second language, knowledge of Shakespeare, etc.

What the playwrights had in common was a deep love of language and a curiosity about the assignment. Not everyone was on board with the idea and I was eager to see how the experiment would be for them. They also pledged to finish the commission within three years.

To celebrate the completion of the translations, we produced a festival in June 2019 in partnership with The Classic Stage Company in New York to hear all 39 of them. Four hundred years ago I think we went to *hear* a play; today we often go to *see* a play. In the staged reading format of the Festival, we heard these plays as if for the first time. The blend of Shakespeare with another writer was seamless and jarring at the same time. Countless actors and audience members told us that the plays were understandable in ways they had never been before.

Now it's time to share the work. We were thrilled when Ayanna Thompson and her colleagues at the Arizona Center for Medieval and Renaissance Studies offered to publish the translations for us.

I ask that you think of these as marking a moment in time.

The editions published in this series are based on the scripts that were used in the Play on! Festival in 2019. For the purpose of the readings, there were cuts allowed and these scripts represent those reading drafts.

The original commission tasked the playwrights and dramaturg to translate the whole play. The requirement of the commission was for two drafts which is enough to put the ball in play. The real fun with these texts is when there are actors, a director, a dramaturg, and the playwright wrestling with them together in a rehearsal room.

The success of a project of this scale depends on the collaboration and contributions of many people. The playwrights and dramaturgs took the assignment seriously and earnestly and were humble and gracious throughout the development of the translations. Sally Cade Holmes and Holmes Productions, our producer since the beginning, provided a steady and calm influence.

We have worked with more than 1,200 artists in the development of these works. We have partnered with more than three dozen theaters and schools. Numerous readings and more than a dozen productions of these translations have been heard and seen in the United States as well as Canada, England, and the Czech Republic.

There is a saying in the theater that 80% of the director's job is taken care of when the production is cast well. Such was my luck when I hired Taylor Bailey, who has overseen every reading and workshop, and was the producer of the Festival in New York. Katie Kennedy has gathered all the essays, and we have been supported by the rest of the Play on Shakespeare team: Kamilah Long, Summer Martin, and Amrita Ramanan.

All of this has come to be because Bill Rauch, then artistic director of the Oregon Shakespeare Festival, said yes when Dave

Hitz pitched the idea to him in 2011. Actually he said, "Hmm, interesting," which I translated to "yes." I am dearly indebted to that 'yes.'

My gratitude to Dave, Ken, and the Hitz Foundation can never be fully expressed. Their generosity, patience, and unwavering belief in what we are doing has given us the confidence to follow the advice of Samuel Beckett: "Ever tried. Ever failed. No matter. Try again. Fail again. Fail better."

Play on!

> Dr. Lue Douthit
> CEO/Creative Director at Play on Shakespeare
> October 2020

WHAT WAS I THINKING?

Julius Caesar
by Nancy Keystone

I work primarily as a director and writer, so when invited to take on the dramaturg role for the Play On! translation of *Julius Caesar*, I was both intrigued and intimidated. A lot of what I love about directing and writing is doing the dramaturgical work, and having directed a good handful of Shakespeare's plays, I've engaged pretty deeply in that process. This proposal summoned me to fully step into those shoes. Shishir Kurup and I had known each other for decades in Los Angeles. I'd been a big fan of his many-tentacled talents as actor, writer, director, and composer, though we'd never had a chance to work together, so I was especially excited to learn that he was the playwright/translator of *Julius Caesar*. What an amazing opportunity to hang out with Shishir and to engage with the play with fresh eyes and ears.

One of the unique features of this assignment — and what made it different from approaching the play as a director — was that we were tasked with a translation of the full play, line-for-line, retaining every element. In other words: no cutting, no moving chunks of text around, no combining characters, no re-ordering scenes, no "fixing," all of which regularly happens in most Shakespeare productions. The job was to actually deal with the most challenging, opaque parts of the text.

TO TRANSLATE, OR NOT: SOME QUESTIONS
From the moment the Play On! idea was announced, there was,

unsurprisingly, a lot of controversy and hand-wringing about messing with Shakespeare's "original," and therefore sacred, texts. I'm more of a "Why not try it?" kind of person, but this mild hysteria prompted me pause. Is this really something we should do? My personal preference when directing a Shakespeare play is to go as close to the source as possible; however, I also appreciate the desire and urgent need for more accessibility. For God's sake, even scholars who spend their whole careers parsing these texts, and actors, directors, and dramaturgs who spend their lives in rehearsal rooms and on stages trying to make sense of what's being said, have never been able to figure out some of it. And no matter how many Shakespeare plays I watch, it takes a good fifteen minutes (and ashamedly longer in these digitally distracted days) for my brain to start making sense of the language. What would it mean to translate these plays?

WHAT IS SHAKESPEARE'S "ORIGINAL," "AUTHENTIC" TEXT?

No one knows. *Julius Caesar* has one of the cleanest trajectories in terms of its provenance; all editions of the play are based on the First Folio, which was printed in 1623 — seven years after Shakespeare's death. There's a fascinating (to me at least!) article[1] about how the Folio was printed, by whom, and under what conditions. The article explains how a couple of actors from Shakespeare's company helped maintain the accuracy of the texts, and how no one knows which manuscripts were used by the printers — whether they were marked-up pages from the actors, a prompt book from a production, a manuscript copy from Shakespeare, or a combination of these. The different variants in the texts may have been the result of printers' errors, their decision to combine two short lines into one long line in order to save paper, or of broken type

---

1 If you like these sorts of rabbit holes, I recommend this article: "Textual Introduction," by John D. Cox. *Internet Shakespeare Editions.* University of Victoria. https://internetshakespeare.uvic.ca/doc/JC_TextIntro/complete/index.html

(e.g., what looks like a period was actually a comma with a broken tail). Not to mention how the many scholarly interpretations have come down to us. *Julius Caesar* is likely one of the most accurately printed plays of the Folio, and even so, hundreds of scholars have spent hundreds of years theorizing, interpreting, and re-editing the play. Just a little of this digging makes it clear that there never has been one, pristine, authentic text, and that brings up a lot of questions about what is "authentic" and "original."

HOW DO I READ A SHAKESPEARE PLAY?

Well, very slowly and disjointedly because I can't read it through without stopping every few words to look up what something means. It turns out, I am simultaneously translating the play as I read it. Because it's really hard to understand, it takes a pile of footnotes, annotations, lexicons, and other sources to even begin to get it.

WHAT DO I EXPERIENCE IN A PRODUCTION OF A SHAKESPEARE PLAY?

It's not Shakespeare's "original," I'll tell you that. I'm gonna go out on a limb and say that 98% of productions of Shakespeare's plays have cut the text, at least a little, and often, a lot. Sometimes multiple versions of the text are combined or there are many more interventions undertaken by the production team. Often there's a glossary in the program, and other resources for the audience, all in service of making the work more understandable, relevant, accessible, and entertaining.

HOW DOES THE REST OF THE NON-ENGLISH-SPEAKING WORLD EXPERIENCE SHAKESPEARE'S PLAYS?

In translation. Spanish, Bengali, Farsi, Dutch, Japanese, Swahili, and Mandarin are only a handful of languages into which Shakespeare's plays have been translated. Upon reflecting on the foreign-language

Shakespeare productions I've seen, I realized that they have been some of the most satisfying and invigorating. In part, I think, because there is more directness and immediacy from the text, through the actors, to the audience, as well as a kind of liberation for the artists.

So, to the question of whether to "translate" Shakespeare or not, I recognized that translation is already at the core of my experience of these plays, whether I'm reading, watching, or working with a team.

TAKING ON THE CHALLENGE

In some senses we were lucky because *Julius Caesar* is one of the shortest plays, clocking in at around 19,700 words (*Hamlet* is over 30,000). It's also one of the clearest in terms of language and action, and as I mentioned, it's one of the least bastardized texts, with fewer versions to reference. Nevertheless, it is still 19,700 words. It's also one of the most famous plays, whose most famous lines are deeply embedded in the culture:

Beware the Ides of March.
(Soothsayer, Act 1, Scene 2)

The fault, dear Brutus, is not in our stars
But in ourselves, that we are underlings.
(Cassius, Act 1, Scene 2)

But, for mine own part, it was Greek to me.
(Caska, Act 1, Scene 2)

Et tu, Brute?
(Caesar, Act 3, Scene 1)

Friends, Romans, countrymen, lend me your ears:
(Antony, Act 3, Scene 2)

This raised issues of audience knowledge and expectation. We needed to be sure that we tackled only the most critical sections and not tamper just because we could. "Do no harm" was Lue's primary admonition. To me, that meant we should try to create the most clarity with the fewest changes.

PROCESS: IN ACTORS WE TRUST

It's one thing to read a play to yourself and an altogether different thing to speak it and hear it. One of the first things we did was arrange a reading with some of our favorite actors in Los Angeles. It was bracing to hear the play with our new task in mind; to listen to how the language and story came out of the actors' mouths — where did it fly, where did it stumble, what was incomprehensible. Everyone had a lot to say after the reading and many of the questions raised that night led us through the rest of the process. It was a great way to dive in.

The bulk of the work happened the following summer, when we were given the opportunity to do a workshop at OSF. We spent a magical week in residence, hashing through the play line-by-line. Shishir decided the best place to work was standing up at the counter in the kitchen area of the fabulous Hay-Patton Rehearsal Center. Honestly, I would have preferred to sit, but it turned out to be just the right place. We stood there reading the play, acting it out, debating, debating, debating — characters' intentions, Shakespeare's intentions, meanings of words and phrases, sounds and rhythms, counting beats, looking things up. My favorite part of the whole process was probably the night we were so carried away that we worked until 3 a.m.

The workshop culminated in a public reading with a terrific company of OSF actors, directed by Killian Directing Fellow, Olivia Espinosa. Fortuitously, some of the cast were in the production of *Julius Caesar,* then playing at OSF, so there was powerful brain trust in the room. During our rehearsals it was especially illuminating to hear from actors who were already so immersed in the play and whose perspectives and questions were deeply informed by that experience. While we'd aimed for a full first draft, as is often the case in the theatre, it was a happy accident that the translation was only about two-thirds complete. Listening to Shishir's work next to some of the untranslated play was really valuable. And there's nothing like having an audience and getting their feedback to show you what work needs to be done.

In the months that followed, Shishir finished the draft and then went on to make many changes and improvements. I think he achieved a piece which maintains Shakespeare's intentions and most of his text, while elegantly and seamlessly weaving in more accessible language. The new translation allows more of Shakespeare's ideas to come through and opens the wonders and blazing relevance of the play to more people — which is what theatre should be.

We were blessed by all the actors and directors who brought their talents, voices, and generosity to the process. I'm grateful to Lue Morgan Douthit for inviting me to the party and for creating this vital program with Dave and Ken Hitz. I'm also grateful to the Hitz Foundation and to Taylor Bailey for making it all go. At every step of the way, there was thought and energy put towards the experience of the Play On! artists to best support our processes. In addition to getting to swim with Shakespeare, we dramaturgs and playwrights were gifted with time to spend together in creative community, sharing delicious meals, questioning, debating, and learning. What a joy and a privilege to get to participate.

Nancy Keystone

July 2021

CHARACTERS IN THE PLAY

(in order of speaking)

FLAVIUS, a tribune

CARPENTER

MURELLUS, a tribune

COBBLER

JULIUS CAESAR, Roman general and statesman and his GHOST

CASKA, a conspirator against Caesar

CALPHURNIA, Caesar's wife

MARK ANTONY, a Roman politician and general, a triumvir after
    Caesar's death

SOOTHSAYER

MARCUS BRUTUS, a conspirator against Caesar

CASSIUS, a conspirator against Caesar

CICERO, a Roman senator

CINNA, a conspirator against Caesar

LUCIUS, Brutus' attendant

DECIUS BRUTUS, a conspirator against Caesar

METELLUS CIMBER, a conspirator against Caesar

TREBONIUS, a conspirator against Caesar

PORTIA, Brutus' wife

CAIUS LIGARIUS, a conspirator against Caesar

SERVANT

PUBLIUS CIMBER, a Roman senator

ARTEMIDORUS, a sophist from Knidos

POPILIUS LENA, a Roman senator

CINNA, a poet

OCTAVIUS CAESAR, a triumvir after Caesar's death

CHARACTERS IN THE PLAY

LEPIDUS, a triumvir after Caesar's death
LUCILIUS, loyal to Brutus and Cassius
PINDARUS, Cassius' bondman
MESSALA, a messenger
VARRUS, loyal to Brutus and Cassius
CLAUDIO, loyal to Brutus and Cassius
TITINIUS, loyal to Brutus and Cassius
YOUNG CATO, Portia's brother
CLITUS, loyal to Brutus and Cassius
DARDANIUS, loyal to Brutus and Cassius
VOLUMNIUS, loyal to Brutus and Cassius
STRATO, loyal to Brutus and Cassius
Other Commoners, Plebeians, Servants, and Soldiers

ACT 1 ◆ SCENE 1

Enter Flavius, Murellus, and certain Commoners onto the stage

FLAVIUS

Go home, you vagabonds, scurry on home!

What's this, a holiday? Now, don't you know

(Being a working man) you oughtn't walk

On a weekday without the markings

Of your vocation. Speak up, what's your job?   5

CARPENTER

Me, sir? A carpenter!

MURELLUS

Where is your level, meas'ring tape, and nail?

Why're you decked out in your Sunday best?

You fella, what's your "calling"?

COBBLER

Well, out of respect for a real worker, sir, I'm what you might   10

call a foot-smith!

MURELLUS

But what's your job? And don't you get too mouthy!

COBBLER

A calling, sir, that keeps me honest, lets me sleep at night,

which is in itself, a heeler of tired soles.

FLAVIUS

What work, you idiot? You nincompoop?   15

COBBLER

Now, pardon sir, don't get mad at me: but if you are mad, sir,

I can heel you.

MURELLUS

Meaning what by that? Heal me, you upstart crow?

1

COBBLER

Well, sir, cobble, you.

FLAVIUS

You're a cobbler, are you? 20

COBBLER

Simon, *ese*! And peachy too! All that I make is made with the awl: I am, sir, a sturgeon to old boots; when they come un-heeled, I reel them.

FLAVIUS

Then why are you not in your shop today?

Why do you drag these men all over town? 25

COBBLER *(on the Q.T.)*

Frankly, sir, to wear out their shoes, to get me more work. But truth be told, sir, we festivate to glimpse Caesar and revel in his triumphs.

MURELLUS

Revel? Why? What conquests does he bring home?

You bricks, you stones, you worse than senseless things! 30

Oh you cold hearted cruel men of Rome!

Remember great Pompey? And all the times

You'd climbed up to the battlements and walls,

To towers and windows even chimney-tops,

Your babies in your arms, and proudly sat 35

The whole damn day, with anxious expectation,

To see great Pompey stride the streets of Rome:

And when you glimpsed his chariot but appear,

Had you not made a cataclysmic howl,

That Tiber trembled to her very banks. 40

And do you now put on your Sunday best?

And do you now eke out a holy day?

And do you now strew flowers in Caesar's way,

That comes in triumph over Pompey's sons?

2

GO HOME!! 45
Run to your houses, fall down on your knees,
Pray to the gods to mitigate the curse
That surely lights on this ingratitude.

FLAVIUS

Go, go, good citizens, and for this ill
Assemble all the poor men of your guild; 50
Draw them to Tiber's banks, and weep your tears
Into the channel, till the lowest stream
Shall kiss the most exalted shores of all.

Exit all the Commoners

See how their simple spirits can't be moved?
They scatter tongue-tied in their guiltiness. 55
You go down that way toward the Capitol.
This way shall I. Disrobe Caesar's statues,
If you should find them decked in decorations.

MURELLUS

Should we do that?
You know it is the Feast of Lupercal. 60

FLAVIUS

It doesn't matter. Don't let images
Be hung with Caesar's trophies. I'll police,
And drive away the rabble from the streets.
These growing feathers plucked from Caesar's wing
Will make him fly an ordinary pitch, 65
Who, left unchecked, would soar above all men,
And keep us all in slavish fearfulness.

Exit all

ACT 1 ♦ SCENE 2

Enter Caesar, Antony for the course, Calphurnia, Portia,
Decius, Cicero, Brutus, Cassius, Caska, a Soothsayer;
after them Murellus and Flavius

CAESAR

Calphurnia.

CASKA

Quiet! Caesar speaks.

CAESAR

Calphurnia.

CALPHURNIA

Here, my lord.

CAESAR

Stand here directly in Antonio's path   5

Where nude he'll run his course. Antonio!

ANTONY

Caesar, my lord.

CAESAR

Remember in your speed, Antonio,

To brush Calphurnia; for the elders say,

That barren wives touched in this holy chase   10

Cast off their sterile curse.

ANTONY

I shan't forget.

When Caesar says, "Do this," it will be done.

CAESAR

Play on! And leave no ceremony out.

Music

SOOTHSAYER

Caesar!   15

CAESAR

Ha! Who calls?

4

CASKA

Hold every noise! Be very, very, quiet!

CAESAR

Who is it from the throng that calls me out?

I hear a tongue more shrill than all the music

Cry "Caesar!" Speak. Caesar is tuned to hear. 20

SOOTHSAYER

Beware the Ides of March.

CAESAR

What man is this?

BRUTUS

An oracle begs you beware the Ides of March.

CAESAR

Place him before me. Let me see his face.

CASSIUS

Fellow, step from the crowd. Look upon Caesar. 25

CAESAR

What do you say to me? Speak once again.

SOOTHSAYER

Beware the Ides of March.

CAESAR

He is a dreamer. Let us leave him. Come!

Cornet … exit all but Brutus and Cassius

CASSIUS

Will you go see the outcome of the run?

BRUTUS

I shan't! 30

CASSIUS

I pray you, do!

BRUTUS

I am not sportive. I do lack some part

Of that exuberance that's in Antony.

Let me not hinder, Cassius, your wishes;
I'll leave you.   35

CASSIUS

Brutus, I have observed you recently.
And find not in your eyes that gentleness
And show of love that I had once relished.
You bear too willful and too stern a hand
Over your friend, that loves you.   40

BRUTUS

Cassius,
Don't be misled. If I've concealed my thoughts,
I turn the contemplation of my brow
Merely upon myself. Displeased am I
Of late with passions of divisive thoughts,   45
Ideas purely native to myself
Which gives some soil, perhaps, to my comportment.
Therefore, let not my good friends be distressed
(Among whose number, Cassius, I count you)
Nor construe any further my neglect   50
Than that, poor Brutus, warring with himself,
Forgets the shows of love to his dear friends.

CASSIUS

Then, Brutus, I have much misjudged your intent,
And as such in this breast of mine have buried
Thoughts of great value, worthy cogitations.   55
Tell me, good Brutus, can you see your face?

BRUTUS

No, Cassius; for the eye can't see itself
But by reflection off some burnished thing.

CASSIUS

'Tis true!
And it is very much lamented, Brutus,   60

6

That you do lack such mirrors that could shine
Your hidden value into your own eyes,
So you might glimpse your own worth: I have heard
Where many of the best revere in Rome,
(Except immortal Caesar) speaking of Brutus,   65
And groaning underneath this age's yoke,
Have wished that noble Brutus had his eyes.

BRUTUS

Into what dangers would you lead me, Cassius,
That you would have me seek into myself
For that which is not in me?   70

CASSIUS

Well then, good Brutus, be prepared to hear.
And since you know you cannot see yourself
So well as by reflection, I, mirror,
Will modestly reveal to your good self
That of yourself, which you yet know not of.   75

Flourish, and roar

BRUTUS

What is this roaring? I fear that the people
Choose Caesar for their king.

CASSIUS

Ah, do you fear it so?
Then I should think you would not have it so.

BRUTUS

I would not, Cassius, yet I love him well.   80
For what do you detain me here so long?
What is it that you would convey to me?
If it pertain toward the general good,
Set honor in one eye, in death the other,
And I will look on both indifferently.   85
For let the gods so bless me, since I love

7

The name of honor more than I fear death.
CASSIUS
    I know that virtue to be in you, Brutus,
    As well as I know your noble face.
    Well, honor is the subject of my story.   90
    I cannot tell what you and other men
    Think of this life; but for my single self,
    I had as soon not be as live to be
    In awe of such a thing as I myself.
    I was born free as Caesar, so were you;   95
    We both have fed as well, and we can both
    Endure the winter's cold as well as he.
    For once, upon a raw and blust'ry day,
    The troubled Tiber chafing at her shores,
    Caesar said to me, "Dare you now, Cassius,   100
    Leap in with me into this angry flood
    And swim to yonder point?" Upon the word,
    Clothed fully as I was, I plunged in
    And urged him follow; which indeed he did.
    The torrent roared, but we demolished it   105
    With lusty sinews, cutting through its roil,
    And stemming it with hearts of disputation.
    But well before we reached the point proposed
    Caesar cried, "Help me, Cassius, or I sink!"
    I, as Aeneas, Rome's great ancestor,   110
    Did from the flames of Troy upon his shoulder
    The old Anchises save, so from the waves of Tiber
    Did I the tired Caesar: and this man
    Is now become a god, and Cassius is
    A wretched creature, and must bend his body   115
    If Caesar carelessly but nod on him?
    He had a fever when he was in Spain,

And when the fit was on him I beheld
How he did shake. It's true, this god did shake:
His craven lips did from their pinkness fly,   120
And that same eye, whose gaze does awe the world,
Did lose its glimmer: I did hear him groan:
Ay, and that tongue of his that pressed the Romans
Mark him, and write his speeches in their books,
"Alas," it cried, "give me some drink, Titinius,"   125
Like a sick girl. My God, it does astound me
A man of such a feeble temper should
So catch the breath of the majestic world
And claim the prize alone.
                    Shout. Flourish.

BRUTUS
Another thund'rous shout?   130
I do believe that these ovations are
For some new honors to be heaped on Caesar.

CASSIUS
Why, man, he stands astride the narrow world
Like a colossus, and we piddling men
Skulk beneath his huge legs and peep about   135
To dig our own dishonorable graves.
Men at some point are masters of their fate.
The fault, dear Brutus, is not in our stars
But in ourselves, that we are underlings.
"Brutus" and "Caesar": What is it about that "Caesar"?   140
Why must that name be sounded more than yours?
Write them together: Yours is as true a name:
Sound them, it does become the mouth as well.
Weigh them, it is as heavy: conjure with 'em,
"Brutus" will fright a spirit as soon as "Caesar."   145
Now in the names of all the gods at once,

Upon what meat does this our Caesar feed
That he is grown so great? Age, be ashamed!
Rome, you have lost your stock of noble bloods!
Now is it Rome indeed, and room enough,   150
When there is in it but only one man.
O, you and I have heard our fathers say
There was a Brutus once would have allowed
A godless devil keep his reign in Rome
Before he would a king.   155

BRUTUS

That you do love me, I am in no doubt:
What you would point me toward, I have a clue:
How I have come to this and of these times
I shortly will unfold. For this moment,
I would not, so with love I shall implore you,   160
Please make no further plea. What you have said
I will consider: what you have to say
I will with patience hear, and find a time
Both apt to hear and answer such grave things.
Till then, my noble friend, chew upon this: 165
Brutus had rather be a foreigner
Than to repute himself a son of Rome
Under these loathe conditions as this time
Will likely lay upon us.

CASSIUS

I am glad   170
That my weak words have struck but this much show
Of fire from Brutus.

Enter Caesar and his train

BRUTUS

The games are done, and Caesar is returning.

CASSIUS

As they pass by, tug Caska by the sleeve,
And he will, in his surly fashion, spew   175
What has emerged note-worthily today.

BRUTUS

I will do so: but look you, Cassius,
The angry spot's on fire on Caesar's brow,
And all the rest like chided schoolboys pout:
Calphurnia's cheek is pale, and Cicero   180
Looks with such ferret and such fiery eyes
Much like we've seen him in the Capitol
Being crossed in quarrel by some senators.

CASSIUS

Caska will tell us what the matter is.

CAESAR

Antonio.   185

ANTONY

Caesar.

CAESAR

Let me have men around me that are fat,
With slicked-back hair, the kind that sleep at night.
That Cassius has a lean and hungry look:
He thinks too much: such men are dangerous.   190

ANTONY

Fear him not, Caesar, he's not dangerous.
He is a noble Roman, even keeled.

CAESAR

Would he were fatter! Though I fear him not:
Yet if Caesar were liable to fear
I do not know the man I should avoid   195
As much as that spare Cassius. He reads much,
He is a great observer, and he sees

11

Straight through the deeds of men. He loves no plays
As you do, Antony; he hears no music.
Seldom he smiles, and smiles in such a way   200
As if he mocked himself and scorned his spirit
For being so moved to smile at anything.
Such men as he are never at heart's peace
While they behold a greater than themselves,
And therefore, they are very dangerous.   205
I'd rather tell you what is to be feared
Than what I fear: for always am I Caesar.
Come on my right hand, for this ear is deaf,
And tell me truly what you think of him.

Sennet

Exit all Caesar and his train

CASKA

You pulled me by the cloak. Would you speak with me?   210

BRUTUS

Yes, Caska, tell us what transpired today
That Caesar looked so sad.

CASKA

Why, you were with him, were you not?

BRUTUS

I would not then ask Caska what transpired.

CASKA

Well, there was a crown offered him; and being offered him,   215
he put it by with the back of his hand, like so, and then the
people started shouting.

BRUTUS

What was the second sound for?

CASKA

Why, for that too.

CASSIUS

They shouted three times: what was the last one for?   220

CASKA

Why, for that also.

BRUTUS

Was the crown offered him thrice?

CASKA

Indeed, it was, and he pushed it off thrice, each time gentler
than the other; and at every putting-by, my honest neighbors
shouted!   225

CASSIUS

Who offered him the crown?

CASKA

Who? Antony!

BRUTUS

Tell us how it played out, gentle Caska.

CASKA

I might as well have monkeys fly out my ass as tell how it
played out. It was pure theatre! I could not abide it! I saw   230
Mark Antony offer him a crown-yet-not-a-crown, really,
'twas one of these coronets — and as I mentioned, he put it
by once; but despite the dumb show, I felt, he would gladly
have had it. So Antony offered it to him again; and he put
it by again. And again, I felt, he was quite loathe to lay his 235
digits off it. And then he offered it the third time; he put the
third time by; and still as he refused it the rabble roared, and
clapped their rough hands, and threw up their sweaty night-
caps, and let out such a bouquet of stinking breath because
Caesar refused the crown that it clearly choked Caesar, for he 240
fainted and fell down at it. And for my own part, I dared not
laugh … for fear of opening my lips and inhaling the bad air.

CASSIUS

But wait, hold on now: What, did Caesar faint?

CASKA

He fell down in the marketplace, foamed at the mouth, and
was speechless.   245

BRUTUS

It's quite likely he has the falling sickness.

CASSIUS

No, Caesar has it not: but you and I,

And honest Caska, we have the falling sickness.

CASKA

I'm not sure what you mean by that, but I am sure Caesar fell
down. If the "hail-thee-fellows" did not applaud and boo him 250
accordingly as he pleased and displeased them, as the players
upon the stage used to do, then call me a monkey's uncle.

BRUTUS

What said he once he came back to his senses?

CASKA

Indeed, before he fell down, when he perceived the loath-
some lemmings were glad he refused the crown, he plucked 255
me open his shirt and offered them his throat to cut. And
had I been a man of working stock, if I would not have taken
him at his word, I might as well have gone to hell among the
scoundrels. And so he fell. When he came to his senses again,
he said, if he had done or said anything amiss, he desired their 260
"worships" to blame it on his infirmity. Three or four "working women" where I stood, cried, "Blessings, good man," and
forgave him with all their hearts. But there's no need to heed
them: if Caesar had stabbed their mothers, they would have
done no less.   265

BRUTUS

And after that he came away morose?

CASKA

Yup.

CASSIUS

Did Cicero say anything?

CASKA

Yup, he spoke Greek.

CASSIUS

And he said?   270

CASKA

If it were my mother tongue you might not call me a liar. But
those that understood him, smiled at one another and shook
their heads; but frankly I say truly it was Greek to me. I have
more news to tell: Murellus and Flavius, are put to silence for
pulling scarves off Caesar's images. Fare you well. There was   275
still more foolery yet, if I could remember it.

CASSIUS

Will you dine with me tomorrow?

CASKA

Sure, if I still draw breath, you're in your right mind, and your
dinner worth the eating.

CASSIUS

Good. I will expect you.   280

CASKA

Do so. Farewell, both.

Exit

BRUTUS

Tomorrow, if you care to speak with me
I will come to your home: or, if you will,
Come to my home, and there I'll wait for you.

CASSIUS

I will do so. Till then, think of the world!   285

Exit Brutus

Well, Brutus, you are noble, yet I see
Your honorable steel may be reshaped
From its volcanic birth. Therefore, it's fitting
That noble minds keep always with their kind;
For who's so firm that cannot be seduced? 290
Caesar resents me, sure, but he loves Brutus.
If I were Brutus now, and he were Cassius,
He could not have swayed me. I will tonight
Throw several missives up at his windows,
As if they came from several citizens, 295
Writings all tending to the great renown
That Rome holds for his name — wherein furtively
Caesar's ambition shall be divulged.
And after this, let Caesar seat him sure,
For we will shake him, or worse days endure. 300

Exit

ACT 1 ◆ SCENE 3

Thunder and lightning
Enter Caska and Cicero

CICERO

Evening, Caska. Did you bring Caesar home?
Why are you breathless, and why do you stare so?

CASKA

Are you not scared, when all the might of earth
Shakes like a thing unfirm? O Cicero,
I have seen tempests when the scolding winds 5
Have hacked the knotty oaks, but never till tonight,
Did I race through a tempest dropping fire.
Either there is a civil strife in heaven,
Or else the world, too brazen with the gods,
Enrages them to send destruction. 10

CICERO

    Why, saw you anything more terrifying?

CASKA

    A common slave — you see him every day —

    Held up his left hand, which did flame and burn

    Like twenty torches joined; and yet this hand,

    Not cognizant of fire, stayed un-scorched.   15

    Besides — I hadn't yet put up my sword —

    Against the Capitol, I met a lion

    Who glowered at me and went surly by

    Without attacking me. And there were drawn

    When these harbingers   20

    Do so align and meet, let men not say,

    "These are the reasons, they are natural":

    For I believe they are prophetic signs

    Toward the climate that is soon to come.

CICERO

    Indeed, it is a strange and puzzling time.   25

    But men construe things to their selfish needs

    Far from the purpose of the things themselves.

    Comes Caesar to the Capitol tomorrow?

CASKA

    He does, for he proposed Antonio

    Send word to you he would be there tomorrow.   30

CICERO

    Good night then, Caska: this disturbed sky

    Is not to walk in.

CASKA

    Farewell, Cicero.

Exit Cicero

Enter Cassius

CASSIUS

Who's there?

CASKA

A Roman. 35

CASSIUS

Caska, by your voice.

CASKA

Your ear is good. Cassius, what a night, huh?

CASSIUS

A very pleasing night to honest men.

CASKA

Whoever knew the heavens threaten so?

CASSIUS

Those that have known this world so full of faults. 40

For my part, I've walked all over the streets,

Submitting myself to this perilous night,

And thus uncloaked as you can see Caska,

Have bared my bosom to Jove's thunderbolt.

CASKA

But why would you attempt to tempt the heavens? 45

It's natural for men to shiver and shake

When angry mighty gods through signals send

Such dreadful omens to astonish us.

CASSIUS

You're foolish, Caska, and those sparks of life

That should be in a Roman you sorely lack 50

Or else you waste them. You look pale, and stare,

And shake with fear, and gawk about in wonder

To see the grave impatience of the heavens.

But if you would consider the real cause

Why all these fires, why all these gliding ghosts, 55

Why birds and beasts stray from their beaten path,

Why all these things change from their normalcy,
Their nature and their primal faculties
To monstrous quality, why, you will find
That heaven has infused them with these spirits   60
To make them instruments of fear and warning
About some monstrous state.
Now could I, Caska, name to you a man
Most like this dreadful night
That thunders, lightens, opens graves, and roars,   65
As does the lion in the Capitol,
A man no mightier than yourself, or me,
In personal action, yet prodigious grown
And fright'ning, as these strange eruptions are.

CASKA

'Tis Caesar that you mean. Is it not, Cassius?   70

CASSIUS

Let it be who it is, for Romans now
Have flesh and limbs not unlike their ancestors:
But woe these times, our fathers' minds are dead.

CASKA

In fact, they say the senators tomorrow
Mean to establish Caesar as a king,   75
And he will wear his crown by sea and land
In every place, save here in Italy.

CASSIUS

I know where I will wear this dagger then:
Cassius from bondage will deliver Cassius.
But life, being weary of these worldly bars   80
Never lacks the power to discharge itself.
If I know this, I'll have the whole world know,
That part of tyranny that I endure
I can shake off at pleasure.

Thunder still

CASKA

So can I. 85

So every minion in his own hand bears

The power to discharge his captivity.

CASSIUS

And why should Caesar be a tyrant then?

Poor man, I know he wouldn't be a wolf

But that he sees that Romans are but sheep. 90

Those in a rush to make a mighty fire

Begin it with weak straws. What trash is Rome?

What rubbish and what refuse? When it serves

For the firewood to illuminate

So vile a thing as Caesar? But, O grief 95

Where have you led me? I perhaps speak this

Before a craven turncoat: then I know

I'll have to answer for it. But I'm armed

And am indifferent to such jeopardy.

CASKA

You speak to Caska, and to such a man 100

Who is no grinning tell-tale. Take my hand.

Be factious for redress to right these wrongs,

And I will place this foot of mine as far

As who goes farthest.

CASSIUS

There's a bargain made. 105

Now know you, Caska, I have swayed already

Some certain of the noblest-minded Romans

To undergo with me an enterprise

Of honorable dangerous consequence;

And I do know by this, they wait for me 110

In Pompey's Porch. As for this fearful night

There is no stir of walking in the streets;
And the appearance of the elements
Are not unlike the work we have in hand,
Most bloody, fiery, and most terrible.   115

Enter Cinna

CASKA

Step back and hide, for here comes one in haste.

CASSIUS

It's Cinna. I do know him by his gait.

He is a friend. Cinna, where haste you so?

CINNA

In search of you. Who's that? Metellus Cimber?

CASSIUS

No, it is Caska, one in union   120

To our attempts. Am I not stayed for, Cinna?

CINNA

Take hand, Caska. What a fearful night is this?

There's two or three of us have seen strange sights.

CASSIUS

Am I not waited for? Tell me.

CINNA

Yes, you are.   125

O Cassius, if you could

But draw the noble Brutus to our party —

CASSIUS

Calm down. Good Cinna, take this paper

And throw this

In at his window. All this done,   130

Go back to Pompey's Porch, where you shall find us.

Is Decius Brutus and Trebonius there?

CINNA

All but Metellus Cimber, and he's gone

21

To seek you at your house. Well, I'll hurry,
And so bestow these papers as you urged me. 135
CASSIUS

That done, return to Pompey's Theatre.

Exit Cinna

Come, Caska, you and I will yet ere day
Meet Brutus at his house. Three parts of him
Is ours already, and the man entire
Upon the next encounter shall be ours. 140
CASKA

Oh, he sits high in all the people's hearts:
And that which would appear offense in us
His noble face, like richest alchemy,
Will change to virtue and to worthiness.
CASSIUS

Him, and his worth, and our great need of him 145
You have rightly deduced. Now let us go,
For it is after midnight, and ere day
We will awake him and make sure he's ours.

Exit all

ACT 2 ◆ SCENE 1

Enter Brutus in his orchard

BRUTUS

What, Lucius, ho?

I cannot, by the progress of the stars

Reckon how near to day — Lucius, I say?

I wish I had the malady of sound sleep.

When, Lucius, when? Awake, I say: Come, Lucius! 5

Enter Lucius

LUCIUS

You called, my lord?

BRUTUS

Place me a candle in my study, Lucius.

When it is lighted, come and fetch me here.

LUCIUS

I will, my lord.

Exit

BRUTUS

It must be by his death: and for my part 10

I have no personal cause to strike at him

But for the greater good. He would be crowned:

How might that change his nature, that's the question.

It is the bright day that brings forth the adder,

And that demands careful walking. Crown him that, 15

And then I fear we'll bless him with a sting

That at his will he may do damage with.

Th'abuse of greatness is when it disjoins

Remorse from power; and truth be told of Caesar

I have not known when his affections swayed 20

23

More than his reason. But it's a common tale
That modesty is young ambition's ladder
To where the upward climber bows his head;
But when he once attains the upmost rung,
He then unto the ladder turns his back,   25
Looks to the clouds, scorning the lower rungs
By which he did ascend. So Caesar may.
Then, lest he may, prevent! And since the quarrel
Is with his future self, not what he is,
Fashion it thus: that what he is, magnified,   30
Would run to these and those extremities.
And therefore think him as a serpent's egg
Once hatched, would as his kind grow troublesome,
So kill him in the shell.

Enter Lucius

LUCIUS

The candle burns within your study, sir.   35
Searching the window for a flint, I found
This paper, thus sealed up, and I am sure
It did not lie there when I went to bed.

Gives him the letter

BRUTUS

Get you to bed again, it is not day.
Is not tomorrow, boy, the first of March?   40

LUCIUS

I know not, sir.

BRUTUS

Look in the calendar and bring me word.

LUCIUS

I will, sir.

Exit

BRUTUS

    The meteors whizzing in the air

    Give so much light that I may read by them.   45

(opens the letter and reads)

    "Brutus, you sleep; awake and see yourself.

    Shall Rome, et cetera. Speak, strike, redress."

    "Brutus, you sleep; awake."

    Such instigations have been often dropped

    Where I have took them up.   50

    "Shall Rome, et cetera." Thus must I piece it out:

    Shall Rome stand under one man's awe? What Rome?

    My ancestors from the streets of Rome did

    The Tarquin drive, when he was crowned king.

    "Speak, strike, redress." Am I solicited then   55

    To speak and strike? O Rome, I promise you,

    If the amends will follow, you'll receive

    Your full entreaty at the hand of Brutus.

               Enter Lucius

LUCIUS

    Sir, March is wasted fifteen days.

               Knock within

BRUTUS

    That's good. Go to the gate: somebody knocks.   60

               Exit Lucius

BRUTUS

    Since Cassius first did whet me 'gainst Caesar

    I have not slept.

    Between the acting of a dreadful thing

    And its first movement, all the interim is

    Like a phantasm or a hideous dream: 65

    Th'unconscious mind and too the sacred flesh

    Unite to take up arms against consciousness,

Like to a little kingdom, suffering
The nature of a bloody civil war.

Enter Lucius

LUCIUS

Sir, it's your brother Cassius at the door,   70
Who does desire to see you.

BRUTUS

Is he alone?

LUCIUS

No, sir, there are more with him.

BRUTUS

Do you know them?

LUCIUS

No, sir. Their hats are covering their ears   75
And half their faces buried in their cloaks,

BRUTUS

Let 'em enter.

Exit Lucius

They are the faction. O conspiracy,
Shamed are you to show your murd'rous brow at night
When evils are most free? O then by day   80
Where will you find a cavern dark enough
To mask your mons'trous visage?

Enter the Conspirators:
Cassius, Caska, Decius, Cinna, Metellus, and Trebonius

CASSIUS

I think we are intruding on your rest.
Good morrow, Brutus. Do we trouble you?

BRUTUS

I have been up this hour, awake all night.   85
Know I these men that come along with you?

CASSIUS

    Yes, every man of them; and no man here

    But honors you, and every one wishes

    You had but that opinion of yourself

    Which every noble Roman carries of you.   90

    This is Trebonius.

BRUTUS

    He is welcome hither.

CASSIUS

    This, Decius Brutus.

BRUTUS

    He is welcome too.

CASSIUS

    This, Caska. This, Cinna. And this, Metellus Cimber.   95

BRUTUS

    They are all welcome.

    What worries have kept you awake tonight

CASSIUS

    May I entreat a word?

They whisper

DECIUS

    Here lies the east. Doth not the day break here?

CASKA

    No.   100

CINNA

    O pardon, sir, it doth, and those grey lines

    That lace the clouds are messengers of light.

CASKA

    You should confess that you are both deceived.

BRUTUS *(comes forward with Cassius)*

    Give me your hands all over, one by one.

CASSIUS

    And let us swear our resolution.   105

BRUTUS

    No, not an oath. If not the grimace of men,

    The sufferance of our souls, the era's abuse;

    If these are weak motives, break off at once,

    And every man back to his idle bed.   110

    So let high-sighted tyranny range on

    Till each man drop by lottery. But if we,

    As I am sure we do, bear fire enough

    To kindle cowards, and to steel with valor

    What need we any spur but our own cause   115

    To prick us to reprisal? What other bond

    Than secret Romans that have spoke the word

    And will not falter? And what other oath,

    Than honesty to honesty engaged,

    That this shall be, or we will fall for it?   120

    Cowards and priests swear as do cautious men,

    Old feeble flesh, and such suffering souls

    That greet abuse: and only men you wouldn't trust

    Would swear to causes bad. But do not stain

    The level virtue of our enterprise,   125

    Nor th'irrepressible strength of our spirits,

    To think that or our cause or our accomplishment

    Did need an oath, when every drop of blood

    That every Roman bears, and nobly bears,

    Is guilty of a sundry bastardy   130

    If he do break the smallest particle

    Of any promise that have passed his lips.

CASSIUS

    But what of Cicero? What will he think?

    I think he will stand very strong with us.

CASKA

Let us not leave him out. 135

CINNA

No, by no means.

METELLUS

O let us have him, for his silver hairs

Will purchase us a good opinion.

It shall be said his judgment ruled our hands.

Our youth and wildness shall be well concealed, 140

But all be buried in his gravity.

BRUTUS

Not Cicero. Let us not split with him,

For he will never follow anything

That other men begin.

CASSIUS

Then leave him out. 145

CASKA

Indeed he is not fit.

DECIUS

Shall no man else be touched but only Caesar?

CASSIUS

Decius, well urged. I think it is not wise

Mark Antony, so well beloved of Caesar,

Should outlive Caesar. We shall find of him 150

A shrewd opponent. And you know his means

If he improve them may well stretch so far

As to imperil us all: which to prevent

Let Antony and Caesar fall together.

BRUTUS

Our course will seem too bloody, Caius Cassius, 155

To cut the head off and then hack the limbs —

Like wrath in death and envy afterwards —

For Antony is but a limb of Caesar.
Let's be sacrificers but not butchers, Caius.
We all stand up against the spirit of Caesar,   160
And in men's spirits you will find no blood.
O that we then could come by Caesar's spirit
And not dismember Caesar! But, alas,
Caesar must bleed for it. And, gentle friends,
Let's kill him boldly, but not wrathfully: 165
Let's carve him as a dish fit for the gods,
Not hew him as a carcass fit for dogs.
And let our hearts, as subtle masters do,
Stir up their servants to an act of rage
And after seem to chide 'em. This will make   170
Our purpose necessary and not envious,
Which so appearing to the common eye,
We shall be called purgers, not murderers.
And for Mark Antony, think not of him,
For he can do no more than Caesar's arm   175
When Caesar's head is off.

CASSIUS
Yet I fear him,
For the conjointed love he bears to Caesar —

BRUTUS
Alas, good Cassius, do not think of him.
If he love Caesar, all that he can do   180
Is hurt himself — and grieve, and die for Caesar.
But that's more than his measure, for he's given
To sports, to wildness and much company.

TREBONIUS
There is no fearing him. Let him not die,
For he will live, and laugh at this hereafter.   185

Clock strikes

BRUTUS

    Peace! Count the clock.

CASSIUS

    The clock hath stricken thrice.

TREBONIUS

    'Tis time to part.

CASSIUS

    But it is doubtful yet

    If Caesar will come forth today or no. 190

    For he of late is superstitious grown,

    Quite from the main opinion he once held

    Of fantasy, of dreams and conjuring.

    It may be these apparent talismans,

    The unaccustomed terror of this night, 195

    And the persuasion of his soothsayers,

    May hold him from the Capitol today.

DECIUS

    Never fear that. If he be so resolved

    I can coerce him: for he loves to hear

    That unicorns may be captured with trees, 200

    And bears with mirrors, elephants in holes,

    Lions with nets, and men with flatterers.

    But when I tell him he hates flatterers,

    He says he does, being then most flattered.

    Let me work. 205

    For I can give his humor the right twist,

    And I will bring him to the Capitol.

CASSIUS

    No, we will all of us go there to fetch him.

BRUTUS

    By the eighth hour. Is that the latest time?

CINNA

Be that the latest time, and fail not then.   210

METELLUS

Caius Ligarius for Caesar has no love,

Who chid him for speaking well of Pompey.

I wonder none of you have thought of him.

BRUTUS

Now, good Metellus, go along by him.

He loves me well, and I have given him reasons.   215

Send him but this way and I'll conscript him.

CASSIUS

Morning has broken. We'll leave you now, Brutus.

And friends, disperse yourselves — but all remember

What you have said, and show yourselves true Romans.

BRUTUS

Good gentlemen, look fresh and merrily.   220

Let not our looks betray our purposes,

But bear it as our Roman actors do,

With rested spirit and steadfast resolve.

And so good morrow to you every one.

Exit all but Brutus

Boy! Lucius! Fast asleep? It is no matter.   225

Enjoy the honey-heavy dew of slumber.

You have no fears, nor no fantasies

Which anxious care spills in the brains of men.

Therefore you sleep so sound.

Enter Portia

PORTIA

Brutus, my lord.   230

BRUTUS

Portia, what means this? Why rise you this hour?

It is not for your health thus to commit

Your weak condition to the raw, cold morning.

PORTIA

Nor for yours neither. You've ungently, Brutus,
Stole from my bed: and yester-eve at supper   235
You suddenly arose, and walked about,
Musing and sighing, with your arms across;
And when I asked you what the matter was
You stared upon me with ungentle looks.
I urged you further: Then you scratched your head   240
And too impatiently stamped down your foot.
Yet I insisted, yet you answered not
But with an angry flutter of your hand
Gave sign for me to leave you. So I did,
Fearing to fortify that impatience   245
Which seemed too much enkindled, nevertheless
Hoping it was but an effect of humor,
Which sometimes has his hour with every man.
It will not let you eat, nor talk, nor sleep;
And could it work so much upon your shape   250
As it has much prevailed on your condition,
I should not know you, Brutus. Dear my lord,
Make me acquainted with your cause of grief.

BRUTUS

I am not well in health, and that is all.

PORTIA

Brutus is wise, and were he not in health,   255
He would embrace the means to come by it.

BRUTUS

Why, so I do. Good Portia, go to bed.

PORTIA

Is Brutus sick, and is it judicious
To walk unlaced and suck up the vapors

Of the dank morning? What, is Brutus sick?   260
And will he steal out of his wholesome bed
To dare the vile contagion of the night?
To add unto his sickness? No, my Brutus.
You have some sick offense within your mind
Which by the right and virtue of my place   265
I ought to know of: and upon my knees
I charm you, by my once commended beauty,
By all your vows of love, and that great vow
Which did amalgamate and make us one,
That you unfold to me, your self, your half,   270
Why you are heavy — and what men tonight
Have had access to you: for here have been
Some six or seven who did hide their faces
Even from darkness.

BRUTUS

Kneel not, gentle Portia.   275

PORTIA

I should not need, if you were gentle Brutus.
Within the bond of marriage, tell me, Brutus,
Is it excluded, I should know no secrets
That do relate to you? Am I your self?
(But as it were), in part or limitation;   280
To keep with you at meals, comfort your bed
And talk to you sometimes? Dwell I but in the suburbs
Of your good pleasure? If it be no more,
Portia is Brutus' harlot, not his wife.

BRUTUS

You are my true and honorable wife,   285
As dear to me as are the crimson drops
That visit my sad heart.

PORTIA

    If this were true, then should I know this secret.

    I grant I am a woman: but also

    A woman that Lord Brutus took to wife.   290

    I grant I am a woman: but as well

    A woman well reputed, Cato's daughter.

    Think you I am no stronger than my sex

    Being so fathered and so husbanded?

    Tell me your counsels. I will not disclose 'em.   295

    I have made strong proof of my constancy,

    Giving myself a voluntary wound

    Here, in the thigh. Can I bear that with patience

    And not my husband's secrets?

BRUTUS

    O ye gods,   300

    Render me worthy of this noble wife!

(knock)

    Listen, one knocks. Portia, go in a while,

    And by and by thy bosom shall partake

    The secrets of my heart.

    All my engagements I will render for you,   305

    All the character of my sad brows.

    Leave me with haste.

Exit Portia

Enter Lucius and Caius Ligarius

    Lucius, who's that knocks?

LUCIUS

    Here is a sick man that would speak with you.

BRUTUS

    Caius Ligarius, that Metellus spoke of.   310

    Boy, stand aside. Caius Ligarius, how?

LIGARIUS

    Accept good morrow from a feeble tongue.

BRUTUS

    O, brave Caius, would you were not sick!

LIGARIUS

    I am not sick, if Brutus have in hand

    Any exploit worthy the name of honor.   315

BRUTUS

    Such an exploit have I in hand, Ligarius,

    Had you a healthful ear to hear of it.

LIGARIUS

    By all the gods that Romans bow before,

    I here discard my sickness. Soul of Rome,

    Brave son, derived from honorable loins,   320

    You like an exorcist have conjured up

    My mortified spirit. Now bid me run

    And I will tackle things impossible,

    Yea, get the better of them! What's to do?

BRUTUS

    A piece of work that will make sick men whole.   325

LIGARIUS

    But are not some whole that we must make sick?

BRUTUS

    That must we also. What it is, my Caius,

    I shall unfold to you as we are going

    To whom it must be done.

LIGARIUS

    Set on your foot,   330

    And with a heart new-fired I follow you,

    To do I know not what: but it sufficeth

    That Brutus leads me on.

Thunder

BRUTUS

Follow me, then.

Exit all

ACT 2 ◆ SCENE 2

Thunder and lightning

Enter Julius Caesar in his nightgown

CAESAR

Nor heaven nor earth have been at peace tonight.

Thrice hath Calphurnia in her sleep cried out,

"Help ho: They murder Caesar." Who's within?

Enter a servant

SERVANT

My lord?

CAESAR

Go bid the priests to make burnt offerings   5

And bring me their opinions of success.

SERVANT

I will, my lord.

Exit

Enter Calphurnia

CALPHURNIA

What mean you, Caesar? Think you to walk forth?

You shall not stir out of your house today.

CAESAR

Caesar shall forth. The things that threaten me   10

Ne'er looked but on my back: when they shall see

The face of Caesar, they shall be vanished.

CALPHURNIA

Caesar, I never stood on ceremony,

Yet now they frighten me. A servant girl,

Beyond the things that we have heard and seen,   15

Recounts most horrid sights seen by watchmen.
A lioness has whelped in the streets,
And graves have yawned and yielded up their dead.
The noise of battle clanging in the air,
Horses do neigh, and dying men did groan,   20
And phantoms shrieked and squealed about the streets.
O Caesar, these things are beyond the pale,
And I do fear them.

CAESAR

What can be avoided
Whose end is purposed by the mighty gods?   25
Yet Caesar shall go forth, for these auguries
Are for the world in general as for Caesar.

CALPHURNIA

When beggars die, there are no comets seen;
The heavens themselves blaze forth the death of princes.

CAESAR

Cowards die many times before their deaths;   30
The valiant never taste of death but once.
Of all the wonders that I yet have heard,
It seems to me most strange that men should fear,
Seeing that death, a necessary end,
Will come when it will come.   35

Enter Servant

What says the Heralds?

SERVANT

They would not have you to stir forth today.
Plucking the entrails of an offering forth,
They could not find a heart within the beast.

CAESAR

The gods do this in shame of cowardice.   40
Caesar should be a beast without a heart

If he should stay at home today for fear.
No, Caesar shall not. Danger knows full well
That Caesar is more dangerous than he.
We are two lions littered in one day,   45
And I the elder and more terrible,
So Caesar shall go forth.

CALPHURNIA

Alas, my lord,
Your wisdom is consumed in confidence.
Do not go forth today. Call it my fear   50
That keeps you in the house, and not your own.
We'll send Mark Antony to the Senate House,
And he shall say you are not well today.
Let me upon my knee be satisfied.

CAESAR

Mark Antony shall say I am not well,   55
And for your mind's peace I will stay at home.

Enter Decius

Here's Decius Brutus. He shall tell them so.

DECIUS

Caesar, all hail. Good morrow, worthy Caesar,
I come to fetch you to the Senate House.

CAESAR

And you are come in very happy time   60
To bear my greeting to the senators,
And tell them that I will not come today.
Cannot is false; and that I dare not, more false.
I will not come today. Tell them so, Decius.

CALPHURNIA

Say he is sick.   65

CAESAR

Shall Caesar send a lie?

Have I in conquest stretched my arms so far
To now be scared to tell old men the truth?
Decius, go tell them Caesar will not come.

DECIUS

Most mighty Caesar, let me know some cause,   70
Lest I be laughed at when I tell them so.

CAESAR

The cause is in my will, I will not come,
That is enough to satisfy the Senate.
But for your private satisfaction,
Because I love you, I will let you know.   75
Calphurnia here, my wife, stays me at home.
She dreamt tonight she saw my statue,
Which like a fountain with a hundred spouts,
Did run pure blood; and many lusty Romans
Came smiling and did bathe their hands in it.   80
And these she fears as warnings and portents
And evils imminent, and on her knee
Has begged that I will stay at home today.

DECIUS

This dream is all interpreted amiss.
It was a vision, fair and fortunate.   85
Your statue spouting blood from many holes
In which so many smiling Romans bathed
Signifies that from you great Rome shall suck
Reviving blood, and that great men shall fight
For tinctures, stains, relics, and knowledge.   90
This by Calphurnia's dream is signified.

CAESAR

And this way have you well expounded it.

DECIUS

I have, when you have heard what else I say.

And know it now: The Senate has concluded
To give this day a crown to mighty Caesar.   95
If you shall send them word you will not come,
Their minds may change. Besides, it were a mock
Apt to be rendered, for someone to say,
"Break up the Senate till another time
When Caesar's wife shall meet with better dreams."   100
If Caesar hide himself, shall they not whisper
"Lo, Caesar is afraid"?
Pardon me, Caesar, but my dear, dear love
For your advancement bids me speak so plain,
And reason over love is liable.   105

CAESAR

How foolish do your fears seem now, Calphurnia!
I am ashamed I did yield to them.
Give me my robe, for I will go.

Enter Brutus, Caius Ligarius, Metellus Cimber,
Caska, Trebonius, Cinna, and Publius

And look where Publius is come to fetch me.

PUBLIUS

Good morrow, Caesar.   110

CAESAR

Welcome, Publius.
What, Brutus, are you stirred so early too?
Good morrow, Caska. Caius Ligarius,
What is't o'clock?

BRUTUS

Caesar, it has struck eight.   115

CAESAR

I thank you for your pains and courtesy.

Enter Antony

See, Antony, that revels long a-nights,

Is notwithstanding up. Good morrow, Antony.

ANTONY

So to most noble Caesar.

CAESAR

Bid them prepare within.   120

I am to blame to be thus waited for.

Now, Cinna. Now, Metellus. Wait, Trebonius,

I have an hour's talk in store for you.

Remember that you call on me today:

Be near me, that I may remember you.   125

TREBONIUS

Caesar, I will.

(aside)

And so near will I be

That your best friends shall wish I had been further.

CAESAR

Good friends, go in, and taste some wine with me,

And we, like friends, will straightway go together.   130

BRUTUS *(aside)*

That every like is not the same, O Caesar,

The heart of Brutus weeps to think upon't.

Exit all

ACT 2 ◆ SCENE 3

Enter Artemidorus reading a paper

ARTEMIDORUS

Caesar, beware of Brutus. Take heed of Cassius. Come not near
Caska. Have an eye to Cinna. Trust not Trebonius. Mark well
Metellus Cimber. Decius Brutus loves thee not. Thou hast
wronged Caius Ligarius. There is but one mind in all these men,
and it is bent against Caesar. If thou beest not immortal, look   5
About you. Security gives way to conspiracy.

The mighty gods defend thee.
Thy lover, Artemidorus.
Here will I stand, till Caesar pass along
And as a suitor will I give him this.   10
My heart laments that virtue cannot live
Beyond the bite of envious rivalry.
If thou read this, O Caesar, thou mayst live;
If not, the Fates with traitors do contrive.

Exit

ACT 2 ◆ SCENE 4

Enter Portia and Lucius

PORTIA

I beg you, boy, race to the Senate House.
Stay not to answer me, but get you gone.
Why do you stay?

LUCIUS

To know my errand, madam.

PORTIA

I would have had you there and here again   5
Ere I can tell you what you should do there.

(aside)

O constancy, be strong upon my side:
Set a huge mountain 'tween my heart and tongue.
I have a man's mind, but a woman's might.
Art thou here yet?   10

LUCIUS

Madam, what should I do?
Run to the Capitol, and nothing else?
Also return to you, and nothing else?

PORTIA

Yes, bring me word, boy, if thy lord look well,

43

For he went sickly forth; and take good note   15
What Caesar does, what suitors press to him.
Wait, boy, what noise is that?

LUCIUS

I hear none, madam.

PORTIA

Well then, listen well!!
I hear a buzzing rumor like a brawl,   20
And the wind brings it from the Capitol.

LUCIUS

In truth, madam, I hear nothing.

Enter the Soothsayer

PORTIA

Come this way, fellow. Where have you been?

SOOTHSAYER

From mine own house, good lady.

PORTIA

You have some suit to Caesar, have you not?   25

SOOTHSAYER

That I have, lady, if it will please Caesar
I shall beseech him to befriend himself.

PORTIA

Why, know you any harm's intended toward him?

SOOTHSAYER

None that I know will be,
Much that I fear may chance.   30
Good morrow to you.

Exit

PORTIA

I must go in. Ay me, how weak a thing
The heart of woman is. O Brutus,
The heavens speed you in your enterprise.

44

Run, Lucius, and commend me to my lord.   35
Say I am merry. Come to me again
And bring me word what he did say to you.

Exit all at separate doors

ACT 3 ◆ SCENE 1

Flourish

Enter Caesar, Brutus, Cassius, Caska, Decius, Metellus,
Trebonius, Cinna, Antony, Lepidus, Artemidorus, Publius,
Popilius Lena, and the Soothsayer

CAESAR

The Ides of March have come.

SOOTHSAYER

Ay, Caesar, but not gone.

ARTEMIDORUS

Hail, Caesar! Read this note.

DECIUS

Trebonius does desire you to o'er-read,

At your best leisure this his humble suit.   5

ARTEMIDORUS

O Caesar, read mine first, for mine's a suit

That touches Caesar nearer. Read it, great Caesar.

CAESAR

What touches me myself shall be last served.

CASSIUS

What, urge you your petitions in the street?

Go to the Capitol.   10

Caesar and his followers move upstage

POPILIUS

I wish your enterprise today may thrive.

CASSIUS

What enterprise, Popilius?

POPILIUS

Fare you well.

47

BRUTUS

    What said Popilius Lena?

CASSIUS

    He wished today our enterprise might thrive: 15

    I fear our purpose is discovered.

BRUTUS

    Look how he makes to Caesar. Observe.

CASSIUS

    Caska, be ready, for we fear prevention.

    Brutus, what shall be done?

BRUTUS

    Cassius, be constant.   20

CASSIUS

    Trebonius knows his time: for look you, Brutus,

    He draws Mark Antony out of the way.

               Exit all Antony and Trebonius

DECIUS

    Where is Metellus Cimber? Let him go

    And presently proffer his suit to Caesar.

BRUTUS

    He is addressed. Press near and second him.   25

CINNA

    Caska, you are the first that rears your hand.

CAESAR

    Are we all ready? What is now wrong

    That Caesar and his Senate must set right?

METELLUS

    Most high, most mighty and most Caesar,

    Metellus Cimber throws before your seat   30

    A humble heart —

CAESAR

    I must prevent you, Cimber:

These kneelings and these bumbling courtesies
Might fire the blood of ordinary men,
And turn what's settled law and first decree   35
Into the games of children. Don't be fooled
To think that Caesar bears such rebel blood
That will be thawed from its brisk quality
With that which melts fools — I mean flattery,
Low-crooked bowing and base puppy fawning.   40
Thy brother by decree is banished.
If you shall bend and pray and fawn for him
I'll boot you like a cur out of my way.
Know, Caesar's not unjust, nor without cause
And will not grant repeal of his sentence.   45

METELLUS

Is there no voice more worthy than my own
To sound more sweetly in great Caesar's ear
For the repealing of my banished brother?

BRUTUS

I kiss your hand, but not in flattery, Caesar,
And do desire that Publius Cimber may   50
Have an immediate freedom of repeal.

CAESAR

What, Brutus?

CASSIUS

Pardon, Caesar: Caesar, pardon.
As low as to your foot does Cassius drop
To beg enfranchisement for Publius Cimber.   55

CAESAR

I could be quite moved, if I were like you:
If I could pray to move, prayers would move me.
But I'm as constant as the northern star,
Of whose true-fixed and resting quality

There is no equal in the firmament.   60
The skies are painted with innumerable sparks;
They are all fire, and every one shines bright;
But there's but one in all doth hold his place.
So in the world: 'tis furnished well with men,
And men are flesh and blood, and indecisive.   65
Yet in that number I do know but one
That unassailable holds on his rank
Unshaked of motion. And that I am he
Let me a little show it even in this,
That I was constant Cimber should be banished   70
And constant still remain to keep him so.

CINNA

O Caesar —

CAESAR

Away! Wilt thou lift up Olympus?

DECIUS

Great Caesar —

CAESAR

Does not Brutus bootless kneel?   75

CASKA

Speak hands for me!

They stab Caesar

CAESAR

Et tu, Brute? — Then fall, Caesar.

Dies

CINNA

Liberty! Freedom! Tyranny is dead!
Run hence, proclaim, cry it about the streets.

CASSIUS

Some to the common pulpits and cry out   80
Liberty, freedom, and enfranchisement!

BRUTUS

People and senators, be not affrighted.

Fly not. Stand still. Ambition's debt is paid.

CASKA

Go to the pulpit, Brutus.

DECIUS

And Cassius too.   85

METELLUS

Stand fast together, lest some friend of Caesar's

Should chance —

BRUTUS

Talk not of standing. Publius, good cheer.

There is no harm intended to your being,

Nor to no Roman else. So tell them, Publius.   90

CASSIUS

And leave us, Publius, lest that the people

Rushing on us, should do your life some mischief.

BRUTUS

Do so, and let no man bear this deed

But we the doers.

Enter Trebonius

CASSIUS

Where is Antony?   95

TREBONIUS

Fled to his house amazed.

Men, wives, and children, stare, cry out, and run,

As it were doomsday!

BRUTUS

Fates, we will know your pleasures.

That we shall die we know; 'tis but the time   100

And drawing days out that men gamble on.

51

CASKA

Why, he that cuts off twenty years of life
Cuts off as many years of fearing death.

BRUTUS

Grant that, and then death is a benefit.
So are we Caesar's friends that have abridged   105
His time, of fearing death. Stoop, Romans, stoop,
And let us bathe our hands in Caesar's blood
Up to the elbows and besmear our swords.
Then walk we forth even to the marketplace,
And waving our red weapons o'er our heads,   110
Let's all cry, "Peace, Freedom, and Liberty!"

CASSIUS

Stoop, then, and wash. How many ages hence
Shall this our lofty scene be acted over
In states unborn and accents yet unknown?

BRUTUS

How many times shall Caesar bleed in sport   115
No worthier than the dust?

CASSIUS

So oft as that shall be,
So often shall the gang of us be called
The men that gave their country liberty.

Enter a servant

BRUTUS

Hold, who comes here? A friend of Antony's.   120

SERVANT

Thus, Brutus, did my master bid me kneel.
Thus did Mark Antony bid me fall down,
And being prostrate thus he bade me say:
If Brutus will reveal that Antony
May safely come to him and be resolved   125

52

How Caesar hath deserved to lie in death,
Mark Antony shall not love Caesar dead
So well as Brutus living, but will follow
The fortunes and affairs of noble Brutus
Throughout the hazards of this untrod moment   130
With all true faith. So says my master, Antony.

BRUTUS

Thy master is a wise and valiant Roman;
I never thought him worse.
Tell him, so please him come unto this place
He shall be satisfied; and by my honor   135
Depart untouched.

Exit Servant

BRUTUS

I know that we shall have him well to friend.

CASSIUS

I wish we may; but yet I have a mind
That fears him much, and my misgivings still
Fall far too close to home.   140

Enter Antony

BRUTUS

But here comes Antony.
Welcome, Mark Antony.

ANTONY

O mighty Caesar! Do you lie so low?
Are all your conquests, glories, your, spoils,
Shrunk to this little measure? Fare you well.   145
I know not, gentlemen, what you intend,
Who else must still be bled, who else is rank.
If I myself, there is no hour so fit
As Caesar's death's hour, nor no instrument
Of half that worth as those your swords, made rich   150

53

With the most noble blood of all this world.
I do beseech you, if you bear me ill,
Now, whilst your bloodied hands do reek and smoke,
Fulfill your pleasure. Live a thousand years,
I shall not find myself so fit to die.   155
No place will please me so, no means of death,
As here by Caesar, and by you cut off,
The movers and the shakers of this age.

BRUTUS

O Antony, beg not your death of us:
Though now we must appear bloody and cruel,   160
As by our hands and this our present act
You see we do, yet you see just our hands
And this, the butcher's business they have done:
Our hearts you see not. They are pitiful,
And pity to the general wrong of Rome —   165
Has done this deed on Caesar. For your part,
To you our swords have rounded tips, Mark Antony.
Our arms both strong and cruel, and our hearts
Of brotherly love, do receive you in,
With all kind love, good thoughts, and reverence.   170

CASSIUS

Your vote shall be as strong as any man's
In the reordering of the new State.

BRUTUS

Only be patient till we have appeased
The ringing throng, beside themselves with fear,
And then we will deliver you the grounds   175
Why I, who did love Caesar when I struck him,
Have thus proceeded.

ANTONY

I don't doubt your wisdom.

Let each man offer me his bloody hand.
First, Marcus Brutus, I will shake with you.   180
Next, Caius Cassius, do I take your hand.
Now, Decius Brutus, yours. Now yours, Metellus.
Yours, Cinna; and my valiant Caska, yours.
Though last, not least in love, yours good Trebonius.
Gentlemen all: Alas, what shall I say?   185
My credit now stands on such slippery ground
That one of two bad ways you must regard me,
Either a coward or a flatterer.
That I did love you, Caesar, O 'tis true.
If then your spirit look upon us now,   190
Shall it not wound you greater than your death
To see your Antony making his peace,
Shaking the bloody fingers of your foes?
O Caesar in the presence of thy corpse,
Had I as many eyes as you have wounds,   195
Weeping as fast as they stream forth your blood,
It would become me better than to join
In terms of friendship with your enemies.
Forgive me, Julius! Here were you cut down, brave hart.
Here did you fall. And here your hunters stand   200
Marked by your death and stained by your blood.
How like a deer, pierced by many princes,
Do you lie here!

CASSIUS

Mark Antony —

ANTONY

Pardon me, Caius Cassius.   205
The enemies of Caesar shall say this:
So, from a friend, it's sober moderation.

CASSIUS

    I don't blame you for praising Caesar so,

    But what compact you mean to have with us?

    Will you be sworn in number of our friends,   210

    Or shall we leave, and not depend on you?

ANTONY

    Therefore I took your hands, but was indeed

    Swayed from the point by looking down on Caesar.

    Friends am I with you all, and love you all,

    Upon this hope, that you shall give me reasons   215

    Why and wherein Caesar was dangerous.

BRUTUS

    Or else were this a savage spectacle.

    Our reasons are so full of good regard

    That were you, Antony, the son of Caesar,

    You would be satisfied.   220

ANTONY

    That's all I seek,

    And am moreover suing that I may

    Produce his body to the marketplace,

    And in the pulpit, as becomes a friend,

    Speak in the order of his funeral.   225

BRUTUS

    You shall, Mark Antony.

CASSIUS

    Brutus, a word with you.

(aside)

    You know not what you do. Do not consent

    That Antony speak in his funeral.

    Know you how much the people may be moved   230

    By that which he will utter.

BRUTUS

   By your pardon:
   I will myself into the pulpit first,
   And show the reason of our Caesar's death.
   What Antony shall speak, I will insist   235
   He speaks by leave and my permission;
   And that we are contented Caesar shall
   Have all true rites and lawful ceremonies,
   It shall advantage more than do us wrong.

CASSIUS

   I know not what may fall. I don't like it.   240

BRUTUS

   Mark Antony, here, you take Caesar's body.
   You shall not in your funeral speech blame us,
   But speak all good you can devise of Caesar,
   And say you do't by our permission:
   Else you shall not have any hand at all   245
   About his funeral. And you shall speak
   In the same pulpit to where I am going,
   After my speech is ended.

ANTONY

   Be it so.
   I do desire no more.   250

BRUTUS

   Prepare the body, then, and follow us.

               Exit all but Antony

ANTONY

   O pardon me, you bleeding piece of earth,
   That I am meek and gentle with these butchers.
   You are the ruins of the noblest man
   That ever lived within the scope of time.   255
   Woe to the hand that shed this costly blood.

Over your wounds now I do prophesy
(Which like mute mouths do ope their ruby lips
As if to beg the voice and utterance of my tongue)
A curse shall light upon the bodies of men: 260
Domestic fury and fierce civil strife
Shall hinder all the parts of Italy:
Blood and destruction shall be so in use,
And deadly objects so familiar,
That mothers shall but smile when they behold 265
Their infants quartered with the hands of war:
All pity choked with custom of deadly deeds,
And Caesar's spirit, spoiling for revenge,
With Ate by his side come hot from hell,
Shall in these confines, with a monarch's voice, 270
Cry havoc and let slip the dogs of war,
That this foul deed shall smell above the earth
With dying men, groaning for burial.
                    Enter Octavius' servant
You serve Octavius Caesar, do you not?
SERVANT
    I do, Mark Antony. 275
ANTONY
    Caesar did write for him to come to Rome.
SERVANT
    He did receive his letters and is coming,
    And bid me say to you by word of mouth —
    O Caesar!
ANTONY
    Your heart is full: Go find a spot and weep. 280
    Passion, I see, is catching, from my eyes,
    Seeing those beads of sorrow stand in yours,
    Bring mine to water. Is your master coming?

SERVANT

He lies tonight within twenty-one miles of Rome.

ANTONY

Ride back with speed and tell him what has chanced.   285

Here is a mourning Rome, a dangerous Rome,

No Rome of safety for Octavius yet.

Hurry back, and tell him so. Yet stay awhile —

You shan't ride back till I have borne this corpse

Into the marketplace. There shall I try   290

In my oration how the people take

The cruel issue of these bloody men,

According to the which you shalt impart

To young Octavius of the state of things.

Lend me your hand.   295

Exit all

ACT 3 ◆ SCENE 2

Enter Brutus and Cassius with the Plebeians

PLEBEIANS

We will be satisfied: let us be satisfied.

PLEBEIAN 3

The noble Brutus is ascended. Silence.

BRUTUS

Be patient till the end.

Romans, countrymen and lovers, hear me for my cause and   5
be silent, so you may hear. Believe me for my honor and take
my honor to heart, so that you may believe me. Be wise when
you will criticize and keep your minds open, that you may
the better judge me. If there are any in this assembly, any dear
friend of Caesar's, to him I say, that Brutus' love to Caesar   10
was no less than his. If then that friend demand why Brutus
rose against Caesar, this is my reason: not that I loved Caesar

less, but that I loved Rome more. Had you rather Caesar were living, and die all slaves, than that Caesar were dead, to live all freemen? As Caesar loved me, I weep for him; as he was 15 fortunate, I rejoice at it; as he was valiant, I honor him; but as he was ambitious, I slew him. There are tears, for his love; joy, for his fortune; honor, for his valor; and death, for his ambition. Who is here so lowly, that would be indentured? If any, speak, for him have I offended. Who is here so rude, 20 that would not be a Roman? If any, speak, for him have I offended. Who is here so vile that will not love his country? If any, speak, for him have I offended. I pause for a reply.

PLEBEIANS

None, Brutus, none!

BRUTUS

Then none have I offended. I have done no more to Caesar, 25 than you shall do to Brutus. The question of his death is enrolle in the Capitol: his glory not inflated, where he was worthy, nor his offenses concealed, for which he suffered death.

Enter Mark Antony with Caesar's body

Here comes his body, mourned by Mark Antony, who, 30 though he had no hand in his death, shall receive the benefit of his dying, a place in the commonwealth, as which of you shall not? With this I depart, that as I slew my best friend for the good of Rome, I have the same dagger for myself, when it shall please my country to need my death. 35

Comes down

PLEBEIANS

Live Brutus, live, live!

PLEBEIAN 1

Bring him with triumph home unto his house.

PLEBEIAN 2

Give him a statue with his ancestors.

PLEBEIAN 3

Let him be Caesar.

PLEBEIAN 4

Caesar's better parts   40

Shall be crowned in Brutus.

PLEBEIAN 1

We'll bring him to his house with shouts and clamors.

BRUTUS

My countrymen.

PLEBEIAN 2

Peace, silence, Brutus speaks.

PLEBEIAN 1

Peace, ho.   45

BRUTUS

Good countrymen, let me depart alone,

And for my sake, stay here with Antony:

Do grace to Caesar's corpse and grace his speech

Tending to Caesar's glories, which Mark Antony,

By our permission, is allowed to make.   50

I do entreat you, not a man depart

Save I alone, till Antony have spoke.

Exit

PLEBEIAN 1

Stay ho, and let us hear Mark Antony.

PLEBEIAN 3

Let him go up into the public chair.

We'll hear him. Noble Antony, go up.   55

ANTONY

For Brutus' sake I am beholding to you.

Goes into the pulpit

PLEBEIAN 4

What does he say of Brutus?

PLEBEIAN 3

He says, for Brutus' sake

He finds himself beholding to us all.

PLEBEIAN 4

'Twere best he speak no harm of Brutus here.   60

PLEBEIAN 1

This Caesar was a tyrant.

PLEBEIAN 3

Nay, that's certain.

We are blest that Rome is rid of him.

PLEBEIAN 2

Peace, let us hear what Antony can say.

ANTONY

You gentle Romans.   65

PLEBEIANS

Peace ho! Let us hear them!

ANTONY

Friends, Romans, countrymen, lend me your ears:

I come to bury Caesar, not to praise him.

The evil that men do lives after them:

The good is oft interred with their bones.   70

So let it be with Caesar. The noble Brutus

Hath told you Caesar was ambitious:

If it were so, it was a grievous fault,

And grievously hath Caesar answered it.

Here, under leave of Brutus and the rest   75

(For Brutus is an honorable man;

So are they all, all honorable men)

I come to speak at Caesar's funeral.

He was my friend, faithful and just to me;

But Brutus says, he was ambitious, 80
And Brutus is an honorable man.
He hath brought many captives home to Rome,
Whose ransoms did the general coffers fill.
Did this in Caesar seem ambitious?
When that the poor have cried, Caesar had wept: 85
Ambition should be made of sterner stuff.
Yet Brutus says, he was ambitious,
And Brutus is an honorable man.
You all did see that on the Lupercal
I thrice presented him a kingly crown, 90
Which he did thrice refuse. Was this ambition?
Yet Brutus says, he was ambitious,
And sure he is an honorable man.
I speak not to disprove what Brutus spoke,
But here I am, to speak what I do know. 95
You all did love him once, not without cause:
What cause withholds you then to mourn for him?
O judgment, thou art fled to brutish beasts
And men have lost their reason. Bear with me.
My heart is in the coffin there with Caesar, 100
And I must pause till it come back to me.

PLEBEIAN 1

I think there is much reason in his sayings.

PLEBEIAN 2

If you consider rightly of the matter,
Caesar has done great wrong.

PLEBEIAN 3

Has he, masters? 105
I fear there will a worse come in his place.

PLEBEIAN 4

Marked you his words? He would not take the crown.

63

Therefore 'tis certain he was not ambitious.

PLEBEIAN 1

If it be true, some will suffer dear for it.

PLEBEIAN 2

Poor soul, his eyes are red as fire weeping.　　　110

PLEBEIAN 3

There's not a nobler man in Rome than Antony.

PLEBEIAN 4

Now listen; he begins again to speak.

ANTONY

Just yesterday the word of Caesar might
Have stood against the world. Now he lies there,
And none so humble to revere him.　　　115
O masters! If I were disposed to stir
Your hearts and minds to mutiny and rage,
I should do Brutus wrong, and Cassius wrong,
Who (you all know) are honorable men.
I will not do them wrong. I rather choose　　　120
To wrong the dead, to wrong myself and you,
Than I would wrong such honorable men.
But here's a parchment, with the seal of Caesar.
I found it in his closet. 'Tis his will.
Let but the people hear this testament —　　　125
Which, pardon me, I do not mean to read —
For they would go and kiss dead Caesar's wounds,
And dip their napkins in his sacred blood,
Yea, beg a hair of him for memory,
And, dying, mention it within their wills,　　　130
Bequeathing it as a rich legacy
Unto their children.

PLEBEIAN 4

Let's hear the will. Read it, Mark Antony.

ACT 3 ◆ SCENE 2

PLEBEIANS

The will, the will. We will hear Caesar's will!

ANTONY

Have patience, gentle friends. I must not read it.   135

It is not fit you know how Caesar loved you.

You are not wood, you are not stones, but men;

And being men, hearing the will of Caesar,

It will inflame you, it will make you mad.

'Tis good you know not that you are his heirs,   140

For if you should, O what would come of it?

PLEBEIAN 4

Read the will, we'll hear it, Antony.

You shall read us the will, Caesar's will.

ANTONY

Will you be patient? Will you stay awhile?

I've gone beyond my place to tell you of it.   145

I fear I wrong the honorable men

Whose daggers have stabbed Caesar: I do fear it.

PLEBEIAN 4

Honorable men? They were traitors.

PLEBEIANS

The will, the testament.

PLEBEIAN 2

They were villains, murderers!! Read the will!!   150

ANTONY

You will compel me then to read the will?

And let me show you him that made the will.

If you have tears, prepare to shed them now.

You all do know this garment. I remember

The first time ever Caesar put it on.   155

'Twas on a summer's evening in his tent,

That day he did defeat the Nervii tribes.

Look, in this place ran Cassius' dagger through:
See what a rent the envious Caska made:
Through this, the well-beloved Brutus stabbed,   160
And as he plucked his cursed steel away,
Mark how the blood of Caesar followed it,
As rushing out of doors to ascertain
If Brutus so unkindly knocked or not;
For Brutus, as you know, was Caesar's angel.   165
Judge, O you gods, how dearly Caesar loved him.
This was the most unkindest cut of all:
For when the noble Caesar saw him stab,
Ingratitude, more strong than traitors' arms,
Quite vanquished him: then burst his mighty heart;   170
And with his mantle muffling up his face,
Even at the base of Pompey's statue,
Which all the while ran red, great Caesar fell.
O what a fall was there, my countrymen!
Then I, and you, and all of us fell down,   175
Whilst bloody treason flourished over us.
O, now you weep, and I perceive you feel
The power of pity: These are gracious drops.
Kind souls, what weep you when you but behold
Our Caesar's clothing wounded? Look you here,   180
Here is himself, scarred as you see with traitors.

PLEBEIAN 2

O noble Caesar!!!

PLEBEIAN 4

O traitors, villains!

PLEBEIAN 1

O most bloody sight!!!

PLEBEIAN 3

We will be revenged!!!   185

PLEBEIANS

    Revenge! About! Seek! Burn! Fire! Kill! Slay!

    Let not a traitor live

ANTONY

    Stay, countrymen.

PLEBEIAN 1

    Peace there, hear the noble Antony!

PLEBEIANS

    We'll hear him, we'll follow him, we'll die with him!!!   190

ANTONY

    Good friends, sweet friends, let me not stir you up

    To such a sudden flood of mutiny:

    They that have done this deed are honorable.

    What private griefs they have, alas, I know not,

    What made them do it: They are wise and honorable   195

    And will no doubt with reasons answer you.

    I come not, friends, to steal away your hearts.

    I am no orator, as Brutus is,

    But, as you know me all, a plain blunt man

    That loved my friend, and that they know full well   200

    That gave me public leave to speak of him.

    For I have neither wit, nor words, nor worth,

    Action, nor utterance, nor the power of speech

    To stir men's blood. I only speak straight on:

    I tell you that which you yourselves do know,   205

    Show you sweet Caesar's wounds, poor poor dumb gapes,

    And bid them speak for me. But were I Brutus,

    And Brutus Antony, that'd be an Antony

    Would ruffle up your spirits and put tongue

    To every wound of Caesar that should move   210

    Even the stones of Rome to rise and mutiny.

PLEBEIANS

We'll mutiny!!!

PLEBEIAN 1

We'll burn the house of Brutus!!!

PLEBEIAN 3

Away then, come, seek the conspirators!!!

ANTONY

Yet hear me, countrymen, yet hear me speak.   215

PLEBEIANS

Peace ho, hear Antony, most noble Antony!

ANTONY

Why, friends, you go to do you know not what.

Wherein hath Caesar thus deserved your loves?

Alas, you know not. I must tell you then.

You have forgot the will I told you of.   220

PLEBEIANS

Most true. The will, let's stay and hear the will!!!

ANTONY

Here is the will, and under Caesar's seal.

To every Roman citizen he gives,

To every single man, seventy-five drachmas.

PLEBEIAN 2

Most noble Caesar, we'll revenge his death!!   225

PLEBEIAN 3

O royal Caesar!!

ANTONY

Hear me with patience.

PLEBEIANS

Peace, ho!!

ANTONY

Moreover, he has left you all his walks,

His private arbors and new-planted orchards,   230

On this side Tiber. He has left them you
And to your heirs forever: common pleasures
To walk abroad and recreate yourselves.
Here was a Caesar: When comes such another?

PLEBEIAN 1

Never, never. Come, away, away!!! 235
We'll burn his body in the holy place,
And with the brands fire the traitors' houses!!!
Take up the body!!!

PLEBEIAN 2

Go fetch fire!!

PLEBEIAN 3

Pluck down benches. 240

PLEBEIAN 4

Pluck down forms, windows, anything.

Exit Plebeians with the body

ANTONY

Now let it work. Mischief, thou art afoot:
Take thou what course thou wilt.

Enter Servant

How now, fellow?

SERVANT

Sir, Octavius is already come to Rome. 245

ANTONY

Where is he?

SERVANT

He and Lepidus are at Caesar's house.

ANTONY

And thither will I straight to visit him.
He comes as I hoped. Fortune is happy
And in this mood will give us anything. 250

69

SERVANT

I heard him say Brutus and Cassius

Have rid like madmen through the gates of Rome.

ANTONY

Perhaps they had some whisper of the people

How I had moved them. Bring me to Octavius.

Exit all

ACT 3 ◆ SCENE 3

Enter Cinna the Poet, and after him the Plebeians

CINNA

I dreamt tonight that I did feast with Caesar,

And things unlucky charge my fantasy.

I have no will to wander forth outdoors,

Yet something leads me forth.

PLEBEIAN 1

What is your name? 5

PLEBEIAN 2

Where are you going?

PLEBEIAN 3

Where do you live?

PLEBEIAN 2

Answer every man directly.

PLEBEIAN 1

Ay, and briefly!!

PLEBEIAN 4

Ay, and wisely. 10

PLEBEIAN 3

Ay, and truly, you were best.

CINNA

What is my name? Whither am I going? Where do I dwell?

Then to answer every man, directly and briefly, wisely and

70

truly: Directly, I am going to Caesar's funeral.

PLEBEIAN 1

As a friend or an enemy?　　　　　　　　　　　　　　　　15

CINNA

As a friend.

PLEBEIAN 2

For your dwelling, briefly!

CINNA

Briefly, I dwell by the Capitol.

PLEBEIAN 3

Your name, sir, truly!!

CINNA

Truly, my name is Cinna.　　　　　　　　　　　　　　　20

PLEBEIAN 1

Tear him to pieces, he's a conspirator.

CINNA

I am Cinna the poet! *Soy Cinna la Poeta!!*

PLEBEIAN 4

Tear him for his bad verses, tear him for his bad verses.

CINNA

I am not Cinna the Conspirator!

PLEBEIAN 4

It doesn't matter; his name's Cinna.　　　　　　　　　25

Pluck but his name out of his heart and send him off!

PLEBEIAN 3

Tear him, tear him!

They set upon him

PLEBEIANS

Come, brands, ho! Firebrands! To Brutus', to Cassius', burn all!

Some to Decius' house, and some to Caska's, some to Ligarius'!

Away, go!　　　　　　　　　　　　　　　　　　　30

Exit all the Plebeians dragging off Cinna

ACT 4 ◆ SCENE 1

Enter Antony, Octavius, and Lepidus

ANTONY

These many, then, shall die; their names are pricked.

OCTAVIUS

Your brother too must die; you consent, Lepidus?

LEPIDUS

I do consent.

OCTAVIUS

Prick him down, Antony.

LEPIDUS

Upon condition Publius shall not live,   5

Who is your sister's son, Mark Antony.

ANTONY

He shall not live. Look, with this mark I damn him.

But, Lepidus, go you to Caesar's house:

Fetch the will hither, and we shall determine

How we might reroute the flow of Caesar's alms.   10

LEPIDUS

What, shall I find you here?

OCTAVIUS

Here, or at the Capitol.

Exit Lepidus

ANTONY

This is a slight, unmeritable man,

Apt to be sent on errands: Is it fit,

The threefold world divided, he should stand   15

One of the three to share it?

OCTAVIUS

    So you heard him,

    And took counsel on who'd be pricked to die

    In our black sentence book and proscription.

ANTONY

    Octavius, I have seen more days than you;   20

    And though we lay these honors on this man

    To ease ourselves of varied sland'rous charges,

    He shall but bear them as the ass bears gold,

    To groan and sweat under th'encumbrance,

    Either led or driven, as we point the way: 25

    And having brought our treasure where we will,

    We then take down his load and set him free,

OCTAVIUS

    You may do your will;

    But he's a tried and fearless soldier.

ANTONY

    So is my horse, Octavius, and for that   30

    I do provide him all the hay he wants.

    He is a creature that I teach to fight,

    To wind, to stop, to run directly on,

    His physical motion governed by my spirit,

    And in some manner, so is Lepidus: 35

    He must be taught, and trained, and bid go forth;

    A barren-spirited fellow.

    Do not talk of him

    But as a property. And now, Octavius,

    Hear greater things. Brutus and Cassius   40

    Are levying powers as we too must do!

    Therefore let our alliance be combined,

    Our best friends coaxed, our means outstretched,

    And let us presently go sit in council,

How covert matters may be best obtained,   45

And open perils surest answered.

OCTAVIUS

Let us do so: for we are at the stake

Surrounded by our many enemies,

And those that smile have in their hearts, I fear,

Millions of mischiefs.   50

Exit all

ACT 4 ◆ **SCENE 2**

Drum. Enter Brutus, Lucilius, and the army.
Titinius and Pindarus meet them.

BRUTUS

What now, Lucilius, is Cassius near?

LUCILIUS

He is at hand, and Pindarus is come

To do you salutation from his master.

BRUTUS

He greets me well. Your master, Pindarus,

Through his own change, or by bad officers,   5

Has given me some worthy cause to wish

Things done, undone: But if he is at hand

I shall have true account.

PINDARUS

I do not doubt

But that my noble master will appear   10

Such as he is, full of regard and honor.

BRUTUS

He is not doubted. A word, Lucilius,

How he received you: let me be resolved.

LUCILIUS

With courtesy and with respect enough,

But not with such familiar instances   15
Nor with such free and friendly conference
As he was wont to do.

BRUTUS

You have described
A hot friend, cooling. Keep in mind, Lucilius,
When love begins to sicken and decay   20
It uses an enforced ceremony.
There are no tricks in plain and simple faith:
But empty men, like horses hot at hand,
Make gallant show and promise of their mettle:

(low march within)

But when they should endure the bloody spur,   25
They drop their crests, and like deceitful jades
Sink in the trial. Comes his army near?

LUCILIUS

They mean this night in Sardis to be quartered.
The greater part, the horse in general,
Are come with Cassius.   30

Enter Cassius and his powers

BRUTUS

Hark, he is arrived.

CASSIUS

Most noble brother, you have done me wrong.

BRUTUS

Judge me, you gods; wrong I my enemies?
And if not so, how could I wrong a brother?

CASSIUS

Brutus, this sober form of yours hides wrongs,   35
And when you do them —

BRUTUS

Cassius, be content.

Speak your griefs softly. We know each other well.
Before the eyes of both our armies here,
Which should perceive nothing but love from us,   40
Let us not quarrel. Bid them move away:
Then in my tent, Cassius, enlarge your griefs,
And I will give you audience.

CASSIUS

Pindarus,
Bid our commanders lead their soldiers off   45
A little from this ground.

BRUTUS

Lucilius, do you as much, and let no man
Come to our tent till we have done our conference.

ACT 4 ◆ SCENE 3

CASSIUS

That you have wronged me doth appear in this:
You have condemned and noted Lucius Pella
For taking bribes here of the Sardians:
Wherein my letters, praying on his side
Because I knew the man, was innocent.   5

BRUTUS

You wronged yourself to write in such a case.

CASSIUS

In such a time as this it is not right
That every small offense should bear censure.

BRUTUS

Let me tell you, Cassius, you yourself
Are much condemned to have an itching palm,   10
To sell and trade your offices for gold
To undeservers.

CASSIUS

I, an itching palm?

You know that you are Brutus that speaks this,

Or by the gods, this speech were else your last. 15

BRUTUS

The name of Cassius honors this corruption,

And chastisement does therefore hide its head.

CASSIUS

Chastisement?

BRUTUS

Remember March, the Ides of March remember:

Did not great Julius bleed for justice's sake? 20

What villain touched his body that did stab

And not for justice? What, shall one of us,

That struck the foremost man of all this world

Stand for supporting robbers: Shall we now

Contaminate our fingers with base bribes, 25

And sell the mighty space of our large honors

For so much trash as may be grasped thus?

I had rather be a dog and bay the moon

Than such a Roman.

CASSIUS

Brutus, bait me not. 30

I'll not endure it. You forget yourself

To hedge me in. I am a soldier, I,

Older in practice, abler than yourself

To make conditions.

BRUTUS

Get out! You are not, Cassius. 35

CASSIUS

I am.

BRUTUS

I say you are not.

CASSIUS

Urge me no more. I shall forget myself.

Have mind upon your health. Tempt me no farther.

BRUTUS

Away, slight man! 40

CASSIUS

Is it so?

BRUTUS

Hear me, for I will speak.

Must I give way and room to your rash choler?

Shall I be frightened when a madman stares?

CASSIUS

O you gods, you gods, must I endure all this? 45

BRUTUS

All this? Yes, more: rage till your proud heart break.

Go show your slaves how ill-tempered you are,

And make your servants tremble. Must I flinch?

Must I observe you? Must I stand and crouch

Under your testy humor? By the gods, 50

You shall digest the venom of your spleen

Though it will split you; for from this day forth,

I'll use you for my mirth, yea for my laughter,

When you are waspish.

CASSIUS

Has it come to this? 55

BRUTUS

You say you are a better soldier:

Then let me see it. Make your boasting true

And it shall please me well. For mine own part,

I shall be glad to learn of noble men.

CASSIUS

    You wrong me every way: you wrong me, Brutus.   60

    I said an elder soldier, not a better.

    Did I say better?

BRUTUS

    If you did, I care not.

CASSIUS

    When Caesar lived he dared not thus have moved me.

BRUTUS

    Peace, peace, you durst not so have tempted him.   65

CASSIUS

    I dared not?

BRUTUS

    No.

CASSIUS

    What, dared not tempt him?

BRUTUS

    For your life, you dare not.

CASSIUS

    Do not presume too much upon my love: 70

    I may do what I shall be sorry for.

BRUTUS

    You have done what you should be sorry for.

    There is no terror, Cassius, in your threats:

    For I am armed so strong in honesty

    That they pass by me as the idle wind,   75

    Which I respect not. I did send to you

    For certain sums of gold, which you denied me,

    For I can raise no money by vile means:

    By heaven, I had rather coin my heart

    And drop my blood for drachmas, than to wring   80

    From the hard hands of peasants their pittances

By any misdirection. I did send
To you for gold to pay my legions,
Which you denied me: Was that done like Cassius?
Should I have answered Caius Cassius so?   85
When Marcus Brutus grows so covetous,
To lock such wretched paltry sums from friends,
Be ready gods with all your thunderbolts,
Dash him to pieces!

CASSIUS

I denied you not.   90

BRUTUS

You did.

CASSIUS

I did not. He was but a fool
That brought my answer back.
Brutus has stabbed my heart.
A friend should bear his friend's infirmities,   95
But Brutus makes mine greater than they are.

BRUTUS

I do not, till you practice them on me.

CASSIUS

You love me not.

BRUTUS

I do not like your faults.

CASSIUS

A friendly eye could never see such faults.   100

BRUTUS

A flatterer's would not, though they do appear
As huge as high Olympus.

CASSIUS

Come, Antony, and young Octavius, come,
Revenge yourselves alone on Cassius,

For Cassius is quite weary of the world: 105
Hated by one he loves, defied by his brother,
Berated like a servant; all his faults displayed,
Inked in a notebook, learned and taught by rote
To throw back at my face. O I could weep
My spirit from my eyes! There is my dagger, 110
And here my naked breast: within, a heart
Dearer than Pluto's mine, richer than gold.
If that you are a Roman, take it forth.
I that denied the gold will give my heart.
Strike as you did at Caesar: For I know, 115
When you hated him worst, you loved him more
Than ever you loved Cassius.

BRUTUS

Sheathe your dagger:
Be angry when you will, it shall have space:
Do what you will, dishonor shall be humor. 120
O Cassius, you are yoked with a lamb
That carries anger as the flint bears fire,
Who, much enforced, shows a hasty spark
And soon is cold again.

CASSIUS

Hath Cassius lived 125
To be but mirth and laughter to his Brutus,
When grief and blood ill-tempered needles him?

BRUTUS

When I spoke that, I was ill-tempered too.

CASSIUS

Do you confess so much? Give me your hand.

BRUTUS

And my heart too. 130

CASSIUS

O Brutus!

BRUTUS

What's the matter?

CASSIUS

Have not you love enough to bear with me,

When that rash humor which my mother gave me

Makes me forgetful? 135

BRUTUS

Yes, Cassius, and from here on

When you are over-earnest with your Brutus,

He'll think your mother chides, and leave you so.

Lucilius and Titinius, task the commanders

Prepare to camp their companies tonight. 140

CASSIUS

And come yourselves, and bring Messala with you

Immediately to us.

Exit Lucilius and Titinius

BRUTUS *(calls)*

Lucius! A bowl of wine.

CASSIUS

I did not think you could have been so angry.

BRUTUS

O Cassius, I am sick from many sorrows. 145

CASSIUS

From your stoic beliefs you glean no use

If you give latitude to chance misfortunes.

BRUTUS

No man bears sorrow better. Portia's dead.

CASSIUS

Ha? Portia?

BRUTUS

    She is dead. 150

CASSIUS

    How 'scaped I murder when I crossed you so?

    O irreplaceable and poignant loss!

    Upon what sickness?

BRUTUS

    Anxious of my absence,

    And grief that young Octavius with Mark Antony 155

    Have made themselves so strong — for with her death

    Those tidings came — with this she fell morose,

    And, with her servants gone, she swallowed hot coals.

CASSIUS

    And died so?

BRUTUS

    Even so. 160

CASSIUS

    O ye immortal gods!

Enter Lucius with wine and candles

BRUTUS

    Speak no more of her: Give me a bowl of wine.

    In this I bury all unkindness, Cassius.

Drinks

CASSIUS

    My heart's been thirsty for that noble pledge.

    Fill, Lucius, till the wine o'er-spill the cup. 165

    I cannot drink enough of Brutus' love.

Exit Lucius

Enter Titinius and Messala

BRUTUS

    Come in, Titinius. Welcome, good Messala.

    Now sit we close about this candle here

And analyze our present pressing needs.

CASSIUS

Portia, are you really gone?   170

BRUTUS

No more, I pray you.

Messala, I have here received letters

That young Octavius and Mark Antony

Come down upon us with a mighty army,

Bending their expedition toward Philippi.   175

MESSALA

Myself have letters of the selfsame tenor.

BRUTUS

With what addition?

MESSALA

That by some legal writs and bills of outlawry

Octavius, Antony, and Lepidus

Have put to death a hundred senators.   180

BRUTUS

Now there our letters do not well agree.

Mine speak of sev'nty senators that died

By their proscriptions, Cicero being one.

CASSIUS

Cicero too?

MESSALA

Cicero is dead,   185

And by that order of proscription.

Had you your letters from your wife, my Lord?

BRUTUS

No, Messala.

MESSALA

Nor nothing in your letters writ of her?

BRUTUS

Nothing, Messala   190

MESSALA

That I think is strange.

BRUTUS

Why ask you?

Hear you news of her in yours?

MESSALA

No, my lord.

BRUTUS

Now, as you are a Roman, tell me true.   195

MESSALA

Then like a Roman bear the truth I tell,

For certain she is dead, and by strange manner.

BRUTUS

Then, farewell, Portia: we all die, Messala:

With meditating that she must die once

I have the patience to endure it now.   200

MESSALA

And thusly great men great losses should endure.

CASSIUS

I have as much of stoic thought as you,

And yet my nature could not bear it so.

BRUTUS

Let's work toward the living. What say you

Of marching to Philippi presently?   205

CASSIUS

I do not think it good.

BRUTUS

Your reason?

CASSIUS

This is it:

It's better that the enemy seek us,
So shall he waste his means, exhaust his soldiers,   210
Doing himself damage, while we, lying still,
Are full of rest, defense, and nimbleness.

BRUTUS

Good reasons must of force give place to better:
The people 'tween Philippi and this ground
Do stand but in a forced affection,   215
For they have grudgingly contributed.
The enemy, marching along by them,
Shall gain by them a fuller number up,
And join refreshed, new-added and encouraged,
From which advantage shall we cut him off   220
If at Philippi we do face him there,
These people at our back.

CASSIUS

Hear me, good brother.

BRUTUS

Under your pardon. You must note beside
That we have tried the utmost of our friends,   225
Our legions are brim full, our cause is ripe.
The enemy increases every day;
We, at the height, are ready to decline.
There is a tide in the affairs of men
Which, taken at the crest, leads on to fortune;   230
Omitted, all the voyage of their life
Is bound in shallows and in miseries.
On such a full sea are we now afloat,
And we must ride the flood for when it serves,
Or lose our ventures.   235

CASSIUS

Then with your will go on.

We'll along ourselves, and meet them at Philippi.

BRUTUS

There is no more to say.

CASSIUS

No more. Good night.

Early tomorrow we'll rise, and depart.   240

Enter Lucius

BRUTUS

Lucius. My gown.

Exit Lucius

Farewell, good Messala.

Good night, Titinius. Noble, noble Cassius,

Good night, and good repose.

CASSIUS

O my dear brother,   245

This was an ill beginning of the night.

Never come such division 'tween our souls.

Let it not, Brutus.

Enter Lucius with the gown

BRUTUS

Everything is well.

CASSIUS

Good night, my lord.   250

BRUTUS

Good night, good brother.

MESSALA

Good night, Lord Brutus.

BRUTUS

Farewell, every one.

Exit Cassius, Titinius, and Messala

Give me the gown. Where is your instrument?

LUCIUS

Here in the tent.   255

BRUTUS

What, you murmur drowsily?

Poor boy, I blame you not; you are over-tired.

Call Claudio and some other of my men.

I'll have them sleep on cushions in my tent.

LUCIUS

Varrus and Claudio!   260

Enter Varrus and Claudio.

VARRUS

Calls my lord?

BRUTUS

I pray you, sirs, lie in my tent and sleep.

It may be I shall wake you by and by

On business to my brother Cassius.

VARRUS

So please you, we will stand and watch your pleasure.   265

BRUTUS

I will not have it so: lie down, good sirs.

If not it may be I shall change my mind.

Look, Lucius, here's the book I sought for so:

I put it in the pocket of my gown.

LUCIUS

I was sure your lordship did not give it me.   270

BRUTUS

Bear with me, good boy, I am much forgetful.

I will not hold you long. If I do live,

I will be good to you.

Let me see, let me see: Is not the leaf turned down

Where I left reading? Here it is I think.   275

Enter the Ghost of Caesar

How ill this candle burns. Ha! Who comes here?
I think it is the weakness of my eyes
That shapes this monstrous apparition.
It comes upon me: Are you anything?
Are you some god, some angel, or some devil,   280
That turns my blood cold, and my hair to stare?
Speak to me what you are.

GHOST

Your evil spirit, Brutus.

BRUTUS

Why come you?

GHOST

To tell you, you shall see me at Philippi.   285

BRUTUS

Well: then I shall see thee again?

GHOST

Ay, at Philippi.

BRUTUS

Why, I will see thee at Philippi, then:

Exit Ghost

Now I have taken heart, you vanish.
Ill spirit, I would hold more talk with thee.   290
Lucius, awake.

LUCIUS

My lord?

BRUTUS

Yes, that you did. Did you see anything?

LUCIUS

Nothing, my lord.

BRUTUS

Sleep again, Lucius. Sirrah Claudio,   295
Fellow, wake up!

VARRUS

My lord?

CLAUDIO

My lord?

BRUTUS

Why did you so cry out, sirs, in your sleep?

BOTH

Did we, my lord?   300

BRUTUS

Ay. Saw you anything?

VARRUS

No, my lord, I saw nothing.

CLAUDIO

Nor I, my lord.

BRUTUS

Go and commend me to my brother Cassius.

Bid him advance his forces before cock's crow   305

And we will follow.

BOTH

It shall be done, my lord.

Exit all

ACT 5 ◆ SCENE 1

Enter Octavius, Antony, and their army.

OCTAVIUS

Now, Antony, our hopes are answered.
You said the enemy would not come down,
But keep the hills and upper regions.
It proves not so: their forces are at hand.
They mean to test us at Philippi here,   5
Prior to what we do demand of them.

ANTONY

Tut, I am in their bosoms and I know
The reason they do it: They really wish
They were some place else, and come down
With fearful bravery, thinking by this face   10
To fasten in our thoughts that they have courage.
But 'tis not so.

> *Enter Brutus, Cassius, and their army:*
> *Lucilius, Titinius, Messala, and others*

BRUTUS

Words before blows: is it so, countrymen?

OCTAVIUS

Not that we love words better, as you do.

BRUTUS

Good words are better than bad strokes, Octavius.   15

ANTONY

In your bad strokes, Brutus, you give good words.
Witness the hole you made in Caesar's heart,
Crying, "Long live! Hail, Caesar!"

CASSIUS

Antony,

The posture of your blows are yet unknown;   20

But, for your words, they rob the Hybla bees

And leave them honeyless.

ANTONY

Not stingless too?

BRUTUS

O yes, and soundless too.

For you have stol'n their buzzing, Antony,   25

And very wisely threat before you sting.

ANTONY

Villains! You did not so, when your vile daggers

Hacked one another in the sides of Caesar.

You showed your teeth like apes, and fawned like hounds,

And bowed like servants, kissing Caesar's feet;   30

Whilst damned Caska, like a cur, behind

Struck Caesar on the neck. O you flatterers!

CASSIUS

Flatterers? Now, Brutus, thank yourself.

This tongue had not offended so today

If Cassius might have ruled.   35

OCTAVIUS

Come, come, the cause. If arguing make us sweat,

The real trial will turn those drops to blood:

Look, I draw a sword against conspirators.

When do you think the sword gets sheathed again?

Never till Caesar's three and thirty wounds   40

Be well avenged, or till another Caesar

Have added slaughter to the sword of traitors.

BRUTUS

Caesar, you cannot die by traitors' hands,

Unless you brought them with you.

OCTAVIUS

So I hope. 45

I was not born to die on Brutus' sword.

BRUTUS

O, if you were the noblest of your strain,

Young man, you couldn't die more honorably.

CASSIUS

A peevish schoolboy, worthless of such honor,

Joined with a bon vivant and party boy. 50

ANTONY

Same old Cassius.

OCTAVIUS

Come, Antony, away.

Defiance, traitors, hurl we in your smile.

If you dare fight today, come to the field;

If not, when you have stomachs. 55

Exit all Octavius, Antony, and army

CASSIUS

Why now, blow wind, swell billow, and swim wood.

The storm is up and all is on the peril.

BRUTUS

Ho, Lucilius, hark, a word with you.

LUCILIUS

My lord.

Brutus speaks apart with Lucilius

CASSIUS

Messala. 60

MESSALA

What says my general?

CASSIUS

Messala,

This is my birthday: as on this very day
Was Cassius born. Give me thy hand, Messala:
Be you my witness, that against my will   65
(As Pompey was) am I compelled to place
Upon one battle all our liberties.

MESSALA

Believe not so.

CASSIUS

I but believe it partly,
For I am fresh of spirit and resolved   70
To meet all perils unwaveringly.

BRUTUS *(comes forward)*

Right, Lucilius.

CASSIUS

Now, most noble Brutus,
The gods today stand friendly, that we may,
Lovers of peace, live onto an old age.   75
But since affairs of men still rest uncertain,
Let's reason with the worst that may befall.
If we do lose this battle, then is this
The very last time we shall speak together.
What are you then determined to do?   80

BRUTUS

Even by the rule of that philosophy
By which I did blame Cato for the death
Which he did give himself — I know not why,
But I do find it cowardly and vile,
For fear of what might fall, so to prevent   85
The time of life.

CASSIUS

Then, if we lose this battle,
You are contented to be led in triumph

Through the streets of Rome?

BRUTUS

No Cassius, no: Think not, thou noble Roman,   90
That ever Brutus will go bound to Rome.
He bears too great a mind. But this same day
Must end that work the Ides of March began;
And whether we shall meet again, I know not:
Therefore our everlasting farewell take: 95
Forever and forever farewell, Cassius.
If we do meet again, why, we shall smile;
If not, why then this parting was well made.

CASSIUS

Forever and forever, farewell, Brutus:
If we do meet again, we'll smile indeed;   100
If not, 'tis true this parting was well made.

BRUTUS

Why then, lead on. O that a man might know
The end of this day's business ere it come:
But it suffices that the day will end,   105
And then the end is known. Come ho, away.

Exit all

ACT 5 ♦ SCENE 2

Alarum

Enter Brutus and Messala

BRUTUS

Ride, ride, Messala, ride, and give these bills
Unto our legions on the other side.

(loud alarum)

Have them advance at once for I can sense
A fearful manner in Octavio's wing,
And sudden push gives us the overthrow.   5

97

Ride, ride, Messala. Let them all come down.

Exit all

ACT 5 ◆ SCENE 3

Alarums

Enter Cassius and Titinius

CASSIUS

O look, Titinius, look, the villains fly:

Myself have to my own turned enemy:

This ensign here of mine was turning back;

I slew the coward and took the flag from him.

TITINIUS

O Cassius, Brutus gave the word too early,   5

Who having some advantage on Octavius

Took it too eagerly: his soldiers fell to loot,

Whilst we by Antony are all enclosed.

Enter Pindarus

PINDARUS

Fly further off, my lord, fly further off,

Mark Antony is in your tents, my Lord: 10

Fly, therefore, noble Cassius, fly far off.

CASSIUS

This hill is far enough. Look, look, Titinius,

Are those my tents where I perceive the fire?

TITINIUS

They are, my lord.

CASSIUS

Titinius, if you love me,   15

Mount you my horse, and hide your spurs in him,

Till he has brought you up to yonder troops

And here again, that I may rest assured

Whether those troops are friend or enemy.

ACT 5 ◆ SCENE 3

TITINIUS

    I will be here again, as quick as thought.   20

               Exit

CASSIUS

    Go, Pindarus, get higher on that hill;

    My eyes were ever marred; observe, Titinius,

    And tell me what you view about the field.

            Exit Pindarus

    This day I breathed my first breath. Time's come round;

    And where I did begin, there shall I end.   25

    My life is run its compass. Pindarus, what news?

PINDARUS *(above)*

    O my lord!

CASSIUS

    What news?

PINDARUS

    Titinius is enclosed round about

    With horsemen, that ride to him on the spur,   30

    Yet he spurs on. Now they are almost on him.

    Now, Titinius. Now some speed: O, he lights too.

    He's taken.

(shout)

    And hark, they shout for joy.

CASSIUS

    Come down, behold no more: 35

    O, coward that I am, to live so long,

    To see my best friend taken before my face.

            Enter Pindarus

    Come closer, Pindarus.

    In Parthia did I take you prisoner,

    And then I swore to you, save for your life,   40

    That whatsoever I did bid you do,

You must attempt it. Come now, keep your oath.
Now be a free man, and with this good sword
That ran through Caesar's bowels, search this bosom.
Stand not to answer: here, take you the hilts,   45
And when my face is covered, as 'tis now,
Guide you the sword — Caesar, thou art revenged
Even with the sword that killed thee.

Pindarus kills him

PINDARUS

So, I am free; yet would not so have been
Dare I have done my will. O Cassius!   50
Far from this country Pindarus shall run,
Where never Roman shall take note of him.

Exit

Enter Titinius and Messala

MESSALA

It is but changed, Titinius: For Octavius
Is overthrown by noble Brutus' power,
As Cassius' legions are by Antony.   55

TITINIUS

These tidings will well comfort Cassius.

MESSALA

Is not that he that lies upon the ground?

TITINIUS

He lies not like the living. O, my heart!

MESSALA

Is not that he?

TITINIUS

No, this was he, Messala,   60
But Cassius is no more. O setting sun:
As in your red rays you do sink tonight,
So in his red blood Cassius' day is done.

Mistrust of my success hath done this deed.

MESSALA

Mistrust of good success hath done this deed.   65

O hateful Error, Melancholy's child,

Why do you show to the apt thoughts of men

The things that are not? O Error, premature,

TITINIUS

What, Pindarus? Where are you, Pindarus?

MESSALA

Seek him, Titinius, whilst I go to meet   70

The noble Brutus, thrusting this report

Into his ears.

TITINIUS

Hurry, Messala.

And I will seek for Pindarus the while.

Exit Messala

Why did you send me forth, brave Cassius?   75

Did I not meet your friends, and did not they

Put on my brows this wreath of victory

And bid me give it you? Did you not hear their shouts?

Alas, you have misconstrued everything.

But hold on, take this garland on your brow;   80

Your Brutus bid me give it you, and I

Will do his bidding. Brutus, come apace,

And see how I regarded Caius Cassius.

By your leave, gods. This is a Roman's part.

Come Cassius' sword, and find Titinius' heart.   85

Dies

Alarum

Enter Brutus, Messala, Young Cato, Strato, Volumnius, and Lucilius

BRUTUS

Where, where, Messala, does his body lie?

MESSALA

There yonder, and Titinius mourning it.

BRUTUS

Titinius' face is upward.

CATO

He is slain.

BRUTUS

O Julius Caesar, you are mighty yet.   90

Your spirit walks abroad and turns our swords

In our own proper entrails.

Low alarums

CATO

Brave Titinius.

Look where he has not crowned dead Cassius.

BRUTUS

Are yet two Romans living such as these?   95

The last of all the Romans, fare you well:

It is impossible that ever Rome

Should breed your equal. Friends, I owe more tears

To this dead man than you shall see me pay.

I shall find time, Cassius: I shall find time.   100

And come, young Cato: let us to the field.

Labio and Flavio set our battles on.

'Tis three o'clock; and, Romans, yet ere night,

We shall try fortune in a second fight.

Exit all

ACT 5 ◆ SCENE 4

Alarum

Enter Brutus, Messala, Young Cato, Lucilius, and Flavius

BRUTUS

Yet, countrymen: O yet, hold up your heads!

Exit fighting, followed by Messala and Flavius

CATO

What bastard does not? Who will go with me?
I will proclaim my name about the field.
I am the son of Marcus Cato, ho!
A foe to tyrants and my country's friend. 5

Enter soldiers and fight

LUCILIUS

And I am Brutus, Marcus Brutus, I!
Brutus, my country's friend: Know me as Brutus!

Young Cato is killed

O young and noble Cato, are you down?
Why now you die as bravely as Titinius,
And may be honored, being Cato's son. 10

SOLDIER 1

Yield, or you die.

LUCILIUS

Only I yield to die.
Kill Brutus, and be honored in his death.

SOLDIER 1

We must not: a noble prisoner!

Enter Antony

SOLDIER 2

Room, ho! Tell Antony, Brutus is caught. 15

SOLDIER 1

I'll tell the news. Here comes the general.
Brutus is caught, Brutus is caught, my lord.

ANTONY

Where is he?
This is not Brutus, friend, but, I assure you,
A prize no less in worth. Keep this man safe; 20
Go on,

And see where Brutus be alive or dead,
And bring us word unto Octavius' tent
How everything is chanced.

Exit all

ACT 5 ◆ SCENE 5

Enter Brutus, Dardanius, Clitus, Strato, and Volumnius

BRUTUS

Come, poor remains of friends, rest on this rock.

CLITUS

Statilius showed the torchlight, but, my lord,
He came not back. He is taken or slain.

BRUTUS

Sit you down, Clitus. Slaying is the word.
It is a deed in fashion. Hark you, Clitus.   5

Whispers

CLITUS

What, I, my lord? No, not for all the world.

BRUTUS

Peace, then. No words.

CLITUS

I'd rather kill myself.

BRUTUS

Hark you, Dardanius.

Whispers

DARDANIUS

Shall I do such a deed?   10

CLITUS

O Dardanius!

DARDANIUS

O Clitus!

CLITUS

What ill request did Brutus make to thee?

DARDANIUS

To kill him, Clitus. Look, he meditates.

CLITUS

Now is that noble vessel full of grief, 15

That it runs over even at his eyes.

BRUTUS

Come here, good Volumnius, do listen.

VOLUMNIUS

What says my lord?

BRUTUS

Why this, Volumnius:

The ghost of Caesar has appeared to me 20

Two several times by night: at Sardis once,

And this last night here in Philippi fields:

I know my hour is come.

VOLUMNIUS

Not so, my lord.

BRUTUS

Nay, I am sure it is, Volumnius. 25

You see the world, Volumnius, how it goes.

Our enemies have beat us to the pit.

(low alarums)

It is more worthy to leap in ourselves

Than linger till they push us. Good Volumnius,

You know that we two went to school together: 30

Even for that our love of old, I pray you

Hold you my sword-hilts whilst I run on it.

VOLUMNIUS

That's not an office for a friend, my lord.

Alarum still

CLITUS

Fly, fly, my lord, there is no tarrying here.

BRUTUS

Farewell to you; and you; and you; Volumnius.   35

Strato, you have been all this while asleep:

Farewell to you too, Strato. Countrymen:

My heart delights that yet in all my life

I found no men who were untrue to me.

I shall have glory by this losing day   40

More than Octavius and Mark Antony

Than this vile conquest shall accumulate.

So fare you well at once, for Brutus' tongue

Has almost ended his life's story:

Night hangs upon mine eyes: my bones would rest,   45

That have much labored to attain this hour.

(alarum)

(Cry within) 'Fly, fly, fly.'

CLITUS

Fly, my lord, fly!

BRUTUS

Go on; I will follow.

> *Exit all Clitus, Dardanius, and Volumnius*

I prithee, Strato, stay you by your lord.   50

You are a fellow of a good respect:

Whose life has had a taste of honor in it.

Hold then my sword, and turn away your face,

While I do run upon it. Will you, Strato?

STRATO

Give me your hand first. Fare you well, my lord.   55

BRUTUS

Farewell, good Strato —

> *Runs on his sword*

Caesar, now be still.
I killed not thee with half so good a will.

Dies. Alarum. Retreat.

Enter Antony, Octavius, Messala, Lucilius, and the army

OCTAVIUS

What man is that?

MESSALA

My master's man. Strato, where is your master?   60

STRATO

Free from the bondage you are in, Messala,
The conquerors can but make a fire of him:
For Brutus only overcame himself,
And no man else hath honor by his death.

LUCILIUS

So Brutus should be found. I thank you, Brutus,   65
That you have proved Lucilius' saying true.

OCTAVIUS

All that served Brutus, I will take them in.

ANTONY

This was the noblest Roman of them all:
All the conspirators save only he
Did what they did in envy of great Caesar.   70
He only with a general honest thought
And common good to all, made one of them.
His life was gentle, and the elements
So mixed in him that nature might stand up
And say to all the world, "This was a man!"   75

OCTAVIUS

According to his virtue let us use him,
With all respect and rites of burial.
Within my tent his bones tonight shall lie,
Most like a soldier, ordered honorably.

So call the field to rest, and let's away,   80
To part the glories of this happy day.
Exit all
END